English Prose Treatises

of

Richard Rolle de Hampole

EARLY ENGLISH TEXT SOCIETY

Original Series, No. 20.

1866, 1921 (for 1920)

Original Series
20

English Prose Treatises

of

Richard Rolle de Hampole

EDITED FROM

ROBERT THORNTON'S MS.

IN THE LIBRARY OF LINCOLN CATHEDRAL

BY

GEORGE G. PERRY, M.A.
PREBENDARY OF LINCOLN AND RECTOR OF WADDINGTON
EDITOR OF 'MORTE ARTHURE'

A new and revised Text and Glossary

LONDON:
PUBLISHED FOR THE EARLY ENGLISH TEXT SOCIETY
BY HUMPHREY MILFORD, OXFORD UNIVERSITY PRESS
AMEN CORNER, E.C.

OXFORD
UNIVERSITY PRESS

Great Clarendon Street, Oxford OX2 6DP
United Kingdom

Oxford University Press is a department of the University of Oxford.
It furthers the University's objective of excellence in research, scholarship,
and education by publishing worldwide. Oxford is a registered trade mark of
Oxford University Press in the UK and in certain other countries

© The Early English Text Society 1866

The moral rights of the authors have been asserted

Database right Oxford University Press (maker)

First Edition published in 1866

All rights reserved. No part of this publication may be reproduced,
stored in a retrieval system, or transmitted, in any form or by any means,
without the prior permission in writing of Oxford University Press,
or as expressly permitted by law, or under terms agreed with the appropriate
reprographics rights organization. Enquiries concerning reproduction
outside the scope of the above should be sent to the Rights Department,
Oxford University Press, at the address above

You must not circulate this book in any other form
and you must impose this same condition on any acquirer

Published in the United States of America by Oxford University Press
198 Madison Avenue, New York, NY 10016, United States of America

British Library Cataloguing in Publication Data
Data available

Library of Congress Cataloging in Publication Data
Data available

Original Series, 20

ISBN 978-0-85-991809-1

PREFATORY NOTE

AMONG the texts left unfinished by Dr. Furnivall was the present re-issue of No. 20, Original Series, of the Society's publications.

As regards the prefatory matter of that issue, a revised text of the *Officium de Sancto Ricardo de Hampole*, the main part of the Preface, had not only been printed off, but had been bound up for circulation among the members, though it would appear never to have been sent out. It is now distributed, as a separate *brochure*, with this re-edition of the text and glossary. In view of the obsolete character of the remaining information in the Preface, it has not been deemed advisable to reprint it at this late date. The text, prepared by Dr. Furnivall, had already been printed off; the glossary, which he had left unfinished, has been revised by Dr. Mabel Day, who has also added the Notes.

I. G.

28 *November*, 1921.

RICHARD ROLLE DE HAMPOLE.

I.

[*Thornton MS., Lincoln Cathedral Library,* leaf 192.]

Of the Vertuȝ of the Haly Name of Ihesu.

Ricardus herimita super versiculo 'Oleum effusum nomen tuum'; in Cantic̀. [I. 3], &c̀.

4 That es on Inglysce 'Oyle owt-ȝettede es thi name'. The name of Ihesu commys in-to the worlde, and als sone it smellys Oyle out-ȝetted. Oyle, it es takyn̄, for ay-lastande saluacyone es hopede. Sothely Ihesu es als mekyłł to be mene als saueoure 8 or helefułł[1]. Thare-fore what[2] menys it, 'Oyle owt-ȝettide es thy nam,' Bot lhesu es thy name? This name es Oyle owte-ȝettyd, For Ihesu, the Worde of God, has tane[3] manes kynde. Ihesu, thow fulfillis in warke that thow es called[4] in name, 12 Sothely sauys [þou] man, þat wham[5] we calle saueoure, Thare-fore Ihesu es thy name. A! A! that wondyrfułł name! A! that delittabyłł name! This es the name þat es abown̄ ałł names; name althirhegeste, witħowtten̄ whilke no[6] man hopes hele. 16 [7] This name es in myn̄ ere heuenly sowne[7], in my mouthe hony-fułł swetnes. Whare-fore[8], na wondire þofe[9] I luf þat name, the whylke[10] gyffes comforthe to me in ałł Angwys. I can noghte pray, I cane noghte hafe mynde, Bot sownnande the[11] nam of 20 Ihesu. I sauyre noghte Ioye that with Ihesu es noghte mengede. Whare-so[12] I be, Whare-so I sytt, What-so I doo, the mynd of the sauoyre of the name Ihesu[13] departis noghte fra my mynde. I haf sett my mynde, I haf sett it als takynnynge appone myn̄

Marginal notes: 'Oil poured forth' is, Iesu, thy name. Oyle, it es takyn̄... By 'poured out' is meant the Incarnation. Iesu is Saviour. This is the highest and most blessed of names. This name will I ever cherish and love.

The readings in the foot-notes are from a MS. of the Treatise in the Harleian Collection, No. 1022, leaf 62, with initial *qw* for Thornton's *wh*.

[1] helpful. [2] qwat. [3] taken. [4] þat at þou art cald.
[5] Sothly man sauys þou qwam. [6] qwilk na.
[7] [7] þis name es swete & Ioyful, gyfand sothfast comforth vnto mans hert, Sothle þo name of ihesu es in my mynde joyus sang, in myn ere heuenly sounde. [8] qwarfor. [9] If. [10] qwilk. [11] þo. [12] qwar-so, &c.
[13] þo mynd of þo name of ihesu.

R. H.   B

I. The Virtues of the Name of Jesus.

My love to it is so strong that it causes me to faint.

arme¹, for luf es strange als dede. Als ded slaas all, Swa lufe ouer-comes all. Ay-lastande lufe has ouer-comemyn² me, noghte for to sla me, bot for to qwykkyn me. Bot it has wondyde me, For it sulde leche me. It has thurghe-fychede my herte, þat 4 merghlyere it be helyde. And now ouer-comen I fayle. Vnnethes I lyfe for Joye. Nerehand I dye; For I suffyce³ noghte in delycyouseste swettnes, And ay to be dronkenede. It falles the flesche may noghte of his vertu noghte defaile ay whils þe⁴ saule 8

Iesu is the source of all my joy.

[†Lf. 192 back.]

in swylk Ioyes is rauyste for to Ioye. Bot when vn-to me swylke Ioye, bot for Ihesu? The nam of Ihesu has taughte me † for to synge, and has lyghtenede my mynde with the hete of vn-made lyghte. Thare-fore I syghe, and crye 'Wha⁵ sall schewe 12 to⁶ þe lufede Ihesu, þat I langwys for lufe?' My flesche has faylede, and my herte meltes⁷ in lufe, ʒarenande Ihesu. All þe herte festenede in þe ʒernynge of Ihesu es turned in-to þe fyre of lufe;

Have mercy then upon me O Iesu!

& with þe swettnes of þe Godhede fullyly es it fillide. Thare- 16 fore, A gude Ihesu, hafe mercy of þis wreche! schewe þe to þis⁸ languessande! be þou leche vn-to þis woundyde! If þou come, I am hale, I fele me noghte seke, bot langwyssande for þi lufe; late my saule takande, sekande þe, Ihesu, whaym⁹ it lufes, with 20 whas⁹ lufe it es takyn, whaym⁹ anely it couaytes. Sothely þe mynd towchede with þe soueraynge swettnes, and es for to waxe

Great is the power of that sweet name.

hate in the lufe of þe makare, qwhyls it enforthis¹⁰ for to halde besyly in it the swetteste name of Ihesu. Sothely fra thythen 24 Inryses¹¹ a gret lufe; and what thynge þat it trewely towches, it rauesche¹² it vtterly to it. It inflawmes þe affeccyone, it byndis þe thoghte, ʒa, & all þe name¹³ it drawes to þe serues¹⁴ of it.

It gives the highest and purest joy.

Sothely, Ihesu, desederabill es thi name, lufabyll and comfort- 28 abyll. ¹⁵ Nane swa swete Ioye may be consaveuede. Nane swa swete sange may be herde. Nane swa swete & delytabyll solace

---

¹ I haue set it as a takenynge opon my hert. als takenynge apon myn Arme.
² ouercomen.
³ I suffice noghte in þis febul flesche for to bere so flowand swetnes of so mykel a mageste, þer skrythes in-to my mynde delyciost swetnes.
⁴ qwylis þo.   ⁵ swa.   ⁶ vnto.   ⁷ has meltyd.   ⁸ þo.   ⁹ qwam, qwas.
¹⁰ enforces.   ¹¹ ryses.   ¹² rauysches.   ¹³ man.   ¹⁴ seruys.
¹⁵ nane so delitabul solace may be had in mynde.

I. The Virtues of the Name of Jesus. 3

may be hade in mynde. Thare-fore, what-so-euer þou bee þat *Therefore whoever* redies the for to lufe Gode, if þou will nowthire be dyssayuede ne *would serve God should* dyssayue, if þou wyll be wysse and noghte vnwysse, if þou will *ever have it in mind.*
4 stande & noghte fall, haue in mynde besely for to halde þe name of Ihesu in þi mynde; and þane thyn̅ Enemy sall fall and þou sall stande, Thyne Enemye sall be made wayke, þou sall be made strange. And if þou will lelely doo this¹, ferre fra drede²,
8 þou sall be gloryus and lowuabyll³ ouercommere. Seke þer-fore the name of Ihesu, and halde it, and for-gette it noghte. Sothely *How infinitely great* na thynge slokynns sa fell flawmes, dystroyes ill⁴ thoghtes, puttes *are its powers.* owte venemous affeccyons, dos a-waye coryous & vayne Oeupa-
12 cyons fra vs. This⁵ name Ihesu, lelely haldyn̅ in mynde, drawes by þe rote vyces, settys vertus, Inlawes⁶ charytee, In-ȝettis⁷ sauoure of heuenely thynges, wastys discorde, reformes pese, Gyffes Inlastande ryste, Dose awaye greuesnes of fleschely desyris,
16 turnes all Erthely thynge to noye, fyllys þe luffande of gastely Ioye. So þat wele it may be saide, '*Et gloriabuntur* Omnes qui* [*MS. gloria-bitur.*] *deligunt nomen tuu*m, *quoniam tu benedices Iusto*,' That es, [Latin in red.] 'All sall Ioye, þat lufes þi name, for þou sall blysse⁸ þe ryghtwyse.' *All shall*
20 Thare-fore þe ryghtewyse has dysseruede to be blyssede, if þe *have joy that love that* name of Ihesu trewly he hase luffede; And þare-fore es⁹ cald *name.* ryghtwyse, For he Enforssede hym trewly to lufe Ihesu. Wharefore, what¹⁰ may de-faile vn-to hym þat couaytes vn-cessandly for
24 to lufe þe name of Ihesu? Sothely he lufes, and he ȝarnes for to *The more one loves the* lufe, For we haue knawen̅ þat þe lufe of Gode standis in swylke *more one desires to* manere þat, In als mekyll als we may¹¹ lufe, þe mare vs langes for *love.* to lufe. For-why¹² it es saide '*Qui edunt me adhuc esurient*¹³, et [Latin in red
28 *qui bibunt me adhuc sciciunt*¹⁴?' þat es to say, 'that¹⁵ ettys me, letters.]* ȝitt hungres thaym; and þay þat drynkes †me, ȝitt thristis [† Leaf 193.] thaym¹⁶.' Thare-fore, beit-selfe, delitabill & couaytabill es þe name of Ihesu, and þe lufe of it. Thare-fore Ioy sall noghte faile¹⁷ vn-to

¹ do lele þis.   ² synne.   ³ alowabul.   ⁴ alle ille.   ⁵ Also this.
⁶ insawes.   ⁷ ȝettes.   ⁸ MS. *repeats* 'þe name for þou sall blysse.'
⁹ eshe.   ¹⁰ perfor qwat.   ¹¹ mare.   ¹² for qwy.   ¹³ esuriunt.
¹⁴ siciunt. And huc is added in margin of Thn. MS., and the Latin verse is repeated at the foot, with 'in Euangelio' added.
¹⁵ þei þat.   ¹⁶ thrist þei.   ¹⁷ want.

I. The Virtues of the Name of Jesus.

Angels desire to look into the virtues of this name.

hym þat couaytes besyly for to lufe hym in whaym Angelis ȝernys for to be-halde. Angelis euer sese, & euer þay ȝerne for to see; and swa are þay fild, þat¹ þaire fillynge duse noghte awaye þaire desyre,² and so þayre desyre duse² noghte awaye

This is infinite joy.

þaire fillynge. This es full Ioye, This es Endles³ Ioye, This es glorious Ioye, þe whylke þe fylde vses⁴ lastandly with-owtten noyc; & if we vse⁵ it, we sall be fyllyde euer withowttyn lessynge. Thare-fore, Ihesu, all sall Ioye þat lufes thi name. Sothely þay sall Ioye nowe, be in-ȝettynge of grace, and in tym to come be syghte of Ioye, and thare-fore þay sall Ioye⁶, For why

He that loves not cannot have joy.

Ioy comes of lufe⁶. Thare-fore, he þat luffes noghte, he sall euer mare be with-owttyn Ioye. Thare-fore many wreches of þe worlde, trowande þam to Ioye with Criste, sall sorowe withowttyn ende. And why⁷? For thay lufede noghte þe name of Ihesu. ⁸What so ȝe doo, if ȝe gyfe all þat ȝe hafe vn-to þe nedy, bot ȝe lufe þe name of Ihesu⁸, ȝe trauelle in vayne. All

His name must be our delight in this life.

anely þay may Ioye in Ihesu þat lufes hym in þis lyfe; and thay þat files⁹ þam with vices & venemous delittes, Na drede þat ne¹⁰ þay ere putt owte of Ioye. Also with all¹¹ þat þe name of Ihesu es helefull, fryutfull & glorious. Þare-fore wha¹² sall haue hele þat lufes it noghte, or wha¹³ sall bere þe frwyte be-fore Criste þat has noghte the floure; and Ioye sall he noghte see That, Ioyeande luffede noghte þe name of Ihesu. The wykkyde sall be don a-waye, þat he see noghte þe Ioye of God. Sothely þe ryghtwyse

The way to find Jesus is

sekys þe Ioye and þe lufe, and þay¹⁴ fynd it in Ihesu, whaym¹⁵ þay luffede. I ȝede abowte be couaytyse¹⁶ of reches, and I fande

Exemplum, Exempla & cetera.

noghte Ihesu. I rane [be¹⁷] the wanntonnes of flesche, and I fand noghte Ihesu. I satt in companyes of worldly myrthe, and I fand noghte Ihesu. In all thire I soghte Ihesu, bot I fand hym noghte, For he lett me wyete by his grace þat he ne es funden in þe lande of softly lyfande. Thare-fore I turnede by anothire

In poverty and penance.

waye, and I rane a-bowte be pouerte, and I fande Ihesu, pure¹⁸

4
4
8
12
16
20
24
28
32

---

¹ of. ² ² þat þeir desire do. ³ endynge. ⁴ qwilk þe fyld vysibul Ioyes.
⁵ vise. ⁶⁻⁶ for þei luf þi name. Sothly warn þei lufd þei myghte not Ioy: & þei þat lufs mare sal Ioy: for qwi Ioy cummes of luf. ⁷ & þat.
⁸⁻⁸ þei. ⁹ fylles. ¹⁰ þat þei are. ¹¹ witte alle. ¹² qwo. ¹³ qwa.
¹⁴ may. ¹⁵ qwam. ¹⁶ about couaytys. ¹⁷ ran be þo wantones. ¹⁸ pore.

II. A Temptation that befell the Hermit Hampole. 5

borne in þe worlde, laid in a crybe and lappid in clathis. I ȝode
by sufferynge of werynes[1], and I fand Ihesu wery in þe way, turment with hu[n]gyre[2], thriste & calde, fild with repreues & blames.
4 I satt by myñ ane, Fleande þe vanytes of þe worlde, and I fande *I fled the world's vani-*
Ihesu in deserte, fastande in þe monte, anely prayande. I rañ *ties, and found Jesus*
by þe payne of [3] penaunce, and I fand Ihesu bowndeñ, scourgede, *in the desert.*
Gyffeñ galle to drynke, naylede to þe Crosse, hyngande in þe
8 Crosse and dyeand in þe Crosse. Thare-fore Ihesu es noghte
fundeñ in reches, bot in pouerte; noghte in delytes, bot in
penance; noghte in wantoñ Ioyeynge, bot in bytter gretynge[4];
noghte emange many, bot in anelynes[5]. Sothely ane euyll[6] mane *The wicked*
12 fyndis noghte Ihesu, for, þare he es, he sekes hym noghte. He *cannot find Him nor know Him.*
enforces hym̃ to seke Ihesu in þe Ioy of þe worlde, whare[7] neuer
he sall be fundeñ. Sothely thare-fore þe nam of Ihesu es hele- *All that de-sire salvation*
full[8], & nedys by-houys be lufed of all couaytande saluacyone. *must love His name.*
16 He couaytes wele hyst saluacyone þat kepis besyly in hym þe *Nota hunc*
name of Ihesu. Sothely I haue na wondyr if þe[9] temptid fall þat *istum passum. [† Lf. 193 bk.]*
puttes noghte þe name of Ihesu in lastande mynde. Sekerly may
he or scho chese[10] to lyfe anely, þat has choseñ þe name of Ihesu to
20 thaire[11] specyalle, For thare may na[12] wykked spyritte noye, þare
Ihesu es mekyll in mynde or is neuennyd[13] in mouthe[14], &c. Explicit.

[II. A Tale of Hampole's Temptation.]
Narracio.
A tale þat Richerde hermet[15] [made].

24 **W**hen[16] I had takeñ my syngulere purpos, & lefte þe seculere *Richard Her-*
habyte, and I be-gane mare to serue God þan mañ, it *mit, in the be-ginning of his*
felle one a nyghte, als I lay in my ryste, in þe begyn- *hermit's life, is tempted by*
nynge of my conuersyone, þare appered to me a full faire *an apparition of a fair young*
28 ȝonge womane, þe whilke I had sene[17] be-fore, & þe whilke[18] luffed *woman.*

---
[1] scharpenesse. [2] hungur. [3] &. [4] bot gretynge. [5] in alones.
[6] ill. [7] qware. [8] helpful. [9] he. [10] he chese. [11] hys.
[12] ne. [13] neuend. [14] þer for it is to hald in my bysele þo name of ihesu.
[15] In the Life of the Hermit (printed in Preface) it is said that this nar-
ration was found after his death—'*in uno libello de suis operibus compilato.*'
In the Harleian MS. it is written as one with the foregoing, and without
title. [16] Qwen. [17] qwilk I had lufd. [18] & sche.

6   *III. A Story of one to whom Schrift did not avail.*

me noght lytiłł¹ in gude lufe. And wheñ² I had be-haldyñ hyre, and I was wondyrde why³ scho com swa on nyghte in þe wyldyrnes, Sodanly, wit*h*owttyñ any mare speche, scho laid hire be-syde me. And wheñ² þat I felyd hir thare, I dred þat scho 4 sulde drawe me to Iuełł, and said þat I wald ryse⁴ & blyse vs in þe name of þe Haly Trynytee. And scho strenyde me so stałł-worthely þat I had no mouthe to speke, ne no hande to styrre;

He discovers that it is the fiend, and vanquishes him by prayer, and the Sign of the Cross.

and wheñ² I sawe þat, I *pe*rceyuede wele þare was⁵ na womane, 8 bot þe deuełł in schappe of womañ. Thare-fore I turnede me to Gode⁵, & wit*h* my mynde I said, 'A, Ih*e*su, how p*re*cyous es thi blude!' makand þe crosse wit*h* my fyngere in my breste: and ałłs faste scho wexe wayke, & sodanly ałł was awaye. And 12

This leads him to love Jesu more ardently.

I thankked Gode þat delyuerd me; & sothely, fra þat tyñ furthe, I forced me for to luf Ih*e*su, and ay þe mare I profette in þe luf of Ih*e*su, þe⁶ swett*er* I fand it, & to þis daye⁷ it went noghte⁸ fra my mynde. Thare-fore, blysside be þe nañ of Ih*e*su 16 in the worlde of worldes! Amen⁹—Amen—**Amen!**
Ih*e*su þe sone of þe glorio*us* virgyne,
Now Lord haue mercy one ałł thyne!—Amen! **Amen!**—
P*ur* charite—Amen.   20

[Follow, 1. '**A** [Latin] **prayere þat þe same Richerd hermet made, þt es beried at Hampulle,**'—*Deus noster refugium, O creator noster*, &c.; 2. '**Ympnus quem composuit** sanc*tus* **Ambrosyus, & est valde bonus,**'—Ih*e*su, 24 nos*t*ra redempcio, amor & desiderium, &c.; Then, on leaf 194,]

III.

[On lf. 194.]   **De in-perfecta contricione.**

Rycharde hermyte reherces a dredfułł tale of vn-p*e*rfitte contrecyone þat a halymane Cesarius tellys in Eusample. 28
He says þat—

The story of the wicked Canon of Paris who made imper-

A ȝonge mane, a chanone at Parys, vn-chastely and delycyously lyfande, and fułł of many synnys, laye seke to þe dede. He schrafe hym of his gret synnys, he hyghte to amende hym, He 32 rescheyuede þe sacrament of þe Autire, and Anoynte hyñ, and

¹ a litel.   ² qwen.   ³ I wondred qwy.   ⁴ ryse vp.
⁵ ⁵ no wom*an* þerfor I t*ur*ned me to god.   ⁶ þe *omitted*.
⁷ & fra þat day.   ⁸ neuer.   ⁹ *The rest omitted*.

IV. A Story of one who was forgiven before Absolution.

swa he dyede. Till his grauynge it semyde als þe ayere gafe *fect shrift and was*
seruese. Eftyr a faa dayes, he apperyde till ane þat was famy- *damned.*
liare till hym in hys lyfe, and sayde þat he was dampnede, for þis
4 Enchesone : ' Þofe I ware,' quod he, 'schreuen, & hyghte to
doo pehance, Me wauntede verray contrycyone, wythowtten þe
whilke, all othere thynges avayles noghte. For-thy, if I
hyghte to lefe my foly, my concyens sayde þat, if I lefede tham,
8 ȝet walde I hafe delyte in myñ alde lyfe. And till þat my
herte heldede mare, and bowghede, Thane to restreyne me
fra all thoghtes þat I knewe agaynes Goddes will. And for-thy
I had na stabyll purpos in gude, na perfite contrycyone, Whare-
12 fore sentence of dampnacyone Felle one me & wente agaynes mee.'

IV.

All-swa he reherces a-nothyre tale of verraye contrecyone, þat þe same clerke † Cesarius says. He tellys [†MS.clreke.]
þat—

16 A scolere at Pares had done many full synnys, þe whylke he *The story of*
hade schame to schryfe hym of. At þe last, gret sorowe of *the scholar of Paris whose*
herte ouercome his schame; and wheñ he was redy to schryfe *great sins*
hym till þe priore of þe Abbay of Saynte Victor, swa mekill con-
20 tricyone was in his herte, Syghynge in his breste, Sobbynge
in his throtte, þat he moghte noghte brynge a worde furthe.
Thane the priore said till hym, 'Gaa and wrytte thy synnes.'
He dyd swa, and come a-gayne to þe pryoure, and gafe hym
24 þat he hadde wretyñ,. For ȝitt he myghte noghte schryfe hym
with mouthe. The prioure saghe the synnys swa grette þat,
thurghe leue of þe scolere, he schewede theym̃ to þe Abbotte, to
hafe conceyle. The Abbotte tuke þat byll þat þay warre *were blotted*
28 wrettyñ Iñ, and lukede thare-one. He fande na thynge wretyñ, *out from the paper on which they*
and sayd to þe prioure, 'What may here be redde, þare noghte *were written.*
es wretyñ ?' That saghe þe pryour, & wondyrde gretly, & saide
'Wyet ȝe þat his synns here warre wretyñ, & I redde thaym̃;
32 Bot now I see þat God has sene hys contrycyone, & forgyfes
hym all his synnes.' þis þe Abbot & þe prioure tolde þe scolere,
and he with gret Ioye thanked God.

V. The Lessons to be learned from the Bee.

V.

Moralia Richardi heremite de natura apis, vnde qualis apis argumentosa. ¶ Apis.

[On lf. 194.]

The three qualities of the bee—
(1) She is [† Lf. 194 bk.] never idle.

The bee has thre kyndis. Ane es, þat scho es neuer ydill, and scho es noghte with thaym þat will noghte wyrke, Bot castys †thaym owte, and puttes thaym awaye.

(2) She weights herself by carrying earth when she flies.

A-nothire es, þat when scho flyes, scho takes erthe in hyr fette þat scho be noghte lyghtly ouer-heghede in the ayere of wynde.

(3) She keeps her wings clean and bright.
Thus rightcous men are never idle.

The thyrde es, þat scho kepes clene and bryghte hire wingez. Thus ryghtwyse men þat lufes God are never in ydyllnes, For owthire þay ere in trauayle, prayand, or thynkande, or redande, or othere gude doande, or with takand ydill men, and schewand thaym worthy to be put fra þe ryste of heuen, For thay will noghte trauayle. Here þay take erthe, þat es, þay halde þam

And hold themselves vile and low and so avoid pride.

selfe vile & erthely, that thay be noghte blawen with þe wynde of vanyte and of pryde. Thay kepe thaire wynges clene, that

And keep the wings of their souls clean by charity.
As the bees fight against those who would rob their honey, so should we against devils. Earthly friends often an impediment to the divine life.

es, þe twa commandementes of charyte þay fulfill in gud concyens, and thay hafe othyre vertus vnblendyde with þe fylthe of syn and vnclene luste. Aristotill sais þat þe bees are feghtande agaynes hym þat will drawe þaire hony fra thaym; Swa sulde we do agaynes deuells þat afforces tham to reue fra vs þe hony of poure lyfe & of grace. For many are þat neuer kane halde þe ordyre of lufe ynesche þaire frendys sybbe or Fremmede, Bot outhire þay lufe þaym ouer mekill, or thay lufe þam ouer lyttill, settand thaire thoghte vnryghtwysely on thaym, or þay lufe thaym ouer lyttill, yf þay doo noghte all as þey wolde till þam. Swylke kane noghte fyghte for thaire hony, For-thy þe deuelle turnes it to wormes, and makes þeire saules ofte sythes full bitter in angwys and tene, and besynes of vayne thoghtes, & oþer wrechidnes, For thay are so heuy in erthely frenchype þat þay may noghte flee in-till þe lufe of Ihesu Criste, in þe wylke þay moghte wele for-gaa þe lufe of all creaturs

As some birds Arestotill fly well and some badly, so is it with men in the service of God.

lyfande in erthe. Whare-fore, accordandly, Arystotill sais þat some fowheles are of gude flyghyng, þat passes fra a land to a-nothire; Some are of ill flyghynge, for heuynes of body and

V. The Bee's Lessons.   VI. The Girl in a Sepulchre.

for þaire neste es noghte ferre fra þe erthe. Thus es it of
thaym̄ þat turnes þam̄ to Godes seruys,—Some are of gude
flyeghynge, for thay flye fra ertho to heuen̄, and rystes thaym̄
4 thare in thoghte, and are fedde in delite of Goddes lufe, and
has thoghte of na lufe of þe worlde. Some are þat kan noghte
flyghe fra þis lande, bot in þe waye late theyre herte ryste, and
delyttes þaym in sere lufes of men̄ and women̄, als þay come &
8 gaa, nowe ane & nowe a-nothire. And in Ihesu Criste þay kan   Some can find
fynde na swettnes; Or if þay any tym̄ fele oghte, it es swa lyttiłł   no sweetness
and swa schorte, for othire thoghtes þat are in thaym̄, þat   in Jesus Christ.
it brynges thaym tiłł na stabylnes. Or þay are lyke tiłł a fowle   They are like
12 þat es callede 'strucyo' or storke, þat has wenges, and it may   the Stork that
noghte flye, for charge of body. Swa þay hafe vndirstandynge,   cannot fly for heaviness.
and fastes and wakes, and semes haly to mens syghte; bot thay
may noghte flye to lufe and contemplacyone of God, þay are so
16 chargede wyth othyre affeccyons and othire vanytes. **Explicit.**

VI

De vita cuiusdam puelle incluse proptter Amorem *Christi.*   [On lf. 194 bk.]

Alswa Heraclides þe clerke telles þat a mayden̄ forsuke   A maiden
† hir Cete, and satte in a sepulcre, and tuke hir mete   shut herself
20 at a lyttiłł hole, ten ȝere. Scho saghe neuer man̄ ne woman̄,   [† Lf. 195.]
ne þay hir face, Bot stode at a hole, and talde why scho was   in a sepulchre
enclosede, And said þat "a ȝonge man was tempede of my   to prevent a
fairehede; For-thy me warre leuere be, als lange als I lyfe,   man sinning by loving her.
24 in þis sepulcre, þan any sawle þat es made til þe lyknes of
Gode, suld perichse by cause of me." And when̄ men askede hire:
how scho myghte swa lyffe, scho said, "fra the begynnynge   She spent her
of the day I gyfe me tiłł praynge tiłł forthe dayes; Thane   days in prayer,
28 I wyrke with handes some thynge; and alswa I wyrke in   in thoughts of martyrs, &c.,
thoghtes, by patryarkes, prophetes, appostilles, Martyrs and
confessours, and by-haldes þaire Ioye. And aftyrwarde I take
my mete. When̄ euen̄ commys, with gret Ioye I lofe my
32 lorde. The ende of my lyfe I habyde in gude hope and thole-   and awaited
modnes": & loo, swa perfitly a woman̄ lyfede! Richard   death in hope.
herymyte reherces þis tale in Ensampiłł.

VII. *An Explanation of the Ten Commandments.*

[Follow, two short Latin pieces; 1. **Richardus heremyta—** *Meliora sunt verbera tua vino,* &c. 2. **Item, inferius idem Richardus,**—*O quam delectabile gaudium et delicatum solacium amare Dei filium,* &c.; then, on leaf 195 back,] 4

VII.

[† Lf. 195 bk.] † **A notabiłł Tretys off the ten Comandementys, Drawen by Richerde, the hermyte off Hampułł.**

¶ Iͤ.
The first Commandment.

The fyrste comandement es 'Thy Lorde God þou sałł loute, and til Hym anely þou sałł serue.' In this comandement 8 es forboden ałł mawmetryse, ałł wychcrafte and charemynge, the wylke may do na remedy tiłł any seknes of man, woman, or beste, For þay erre þe snarrys of þe deuelle, by þe whilke he afforces hym to dyssayue mankynde. Alswa in þis 12 commandemente es forbodyn to gyffe trouthe tiłł socerye or tiłł dyuynyngeȝ by sternys, or by dremys, or by any swylke thynges. Astronomyenes by-haldes þe daye and þe houre, and þe poynte þat man es borne In, and vndyr whylke syngne he es borne, 16 and þe poynte þat he begynnes to be In; and by þire syngnes and oþer, þay saye þat þay say that sałł be-fałł þe man aftyrwarde; Bot theyre errowre es reproffede of haly doctours. Haly crosses men sałł lowte, For thay are in syngne of Cryste 20 crucyfiede. To ymages es þe louynge þat es tiłł thaym of whaym þaire are þe ymageȝ, For þat Entent anely þaire are for to lowte.

Forbids witchcraft, sorcery, divining, and astrology.

Men may reverence holy crosses and images.

¶ ijͤ.
The second Commandment (third in Decalogue).
Forbids vain and wicked oaths.

The tothire comandement es 'þou sałł noghte take þe name 24 of God in vayne.' Here is forboden athe with-owtten cheson. He þat neuenes God & sweris fals, dispyse[s] God. In thre maners mane may syn in swerynge; That es, if he swere agayne his concyence, or if he swere be Cryste wondes or blude, 28 That es euermare gret syn, þofe it be sothe þat he sweris, For it sounes in irreu[er]ence of Ihesu Cryste. Also if he com agaynes his athe, noght fulfilland þat he has sworne. The nam

VII. An Explanation of the Ten Commandments. 11

of Gode es takyñ in vayne one many maners : with herte, with *The name of God taken in vain in many manners.*
mouthe, with werke. With herte, takes false crystyñ meñ it in
vayne, þat rescheyues þe sacrement with-owtteñ grace in sawle.
4 With mouthe es it tane in vayne, with all athes brekynge, of new
prechynge þat es vanyte and vndevocyone; prayere, when we *New preaching, formal prayer, and hypocrisy.*
honour God with oure lyppys, and oure hertys erre ferre fra Hym.
With werke, ypocrittes takes Goddes nam in vayne, For they
8 feyne gud dede with-owtteñ, and þey erre with-owtteñ charyte
and vertue and force of sawle to stand agayne all ill styrrynges.

The thirde commandement es 'Vmbethynke the þat thow halowe *¶ iij*. The third (fourth) Commandment. Its general meaning. Special meaning for contemplative men.*
þi halydaye.' This commandement may be takyñ in thre
12 maneres. Firste generally, þat we sesse of all vyces þat lettys
deuocyone to God in prayenge and thynkynge. The thyrde[1] es
specyall, als in contemplaytyfe meñ þat departis þaym̄ fra all
werldly thynges, swa þat þey hally gyfe þaym̄ till God. The
16 fyrste manere es nedfull vs to do; The tothire we awe to do;
The thirde es perfeccyone. For-thi, one þe halydaye, men awe,
als God byddys, to lefe all syñ, and do na werke þat lettis
thaym̄ to gyffe þaire herte to Godd, thatt þay halowe þe daye
20 in ryst, and deuocyone, and dedys of charyte.

The ferthe comandement es 'Honoure thy fadyre and þi *¶ iiij*. The fourth (fifth) Commandment. Duty to parents bodily and ghostly.*
modyre.' That es, in twa thynges, þat es, bodyly and gastely.
Bodyly, in sustenance, þat þay be helpede and sustaynede in þaire
24 elde, and when þay are vnmyghtty of þaym̄ selfe. Gastely, in
reuerence and bouxomnes, þat þay say to þam̄ na wordes of
myssawe, ne vnhoneste, ne of displesançe, vnauyssedly, Bot serue
þam̄ mekely, and gladly and lawlyly, þat þay may wyñ þat
28 Godde hyghte to swylke barnes þat es laude of lyghte. And if *If they are dead their souls must be helped by alms-deeds.*
þay be dede, thaym awe to helpe þaire sawles with almous dedes
and prayers.

The fifte commandement † es, þat ' thow slaa na mañ, nowthire *¶ v*. [† Lf. 196.] The fifth (sixth) Commandment.*
32 with assente, ne with werke, ne with worde or fauour.' And also
here es forbodeñ vn-ryghtewyse hurtynge of any persoñ. Thay
are slaers gastely, þat will noghte feede þe pouer in nede, and *Spiritual murderers.*
þat defames men, and þat confoundes Innocentys.

[1] The second, or 'tothire,' is omitted.

VII. An Explanation of the Ten Commandments.

¶ vj. The sixth(7th) Commandment. Forbids all manner of pollution.

The sexte commandement es, 'Thow salt be na lichoure'; þat es, thow salt haue na man or woman Bot þat þou has taken in fourme of Haly Kyrke. Alswa here es forboden all maner of wilfull pollusyone procurede one any maner agaynes kyndly oys or oþer-gates.

¶ vij. The seventh (eighth) Commandment. All cheating and imposture forbidden.

The seuende commandement, es 'Thow salt noghte do na thyfte.' In the whylke es forboden all manere of withdraweynge of oþer men thynges wrangwysely, agaynes þaire wyll þat aghte it, Bot if it ware in tyme of maste nede, when all thynges erre comone. Also here es forboden gillery of weghte or of tale, or of mett or of mesure, or thorow okyre, or violence, or drede, als bedells or foresters duse, and mynystyrs of þe kynge, or thurghe extorcyone, als lordes duse.

¶ viij. The eighth (ninth) Commandment. All lying is not deadly sin.

The aughten commandement es, that 'thow salt noghte bere false wyttnes agaynes thi neghteboure,' als in assys, or cause of matremoyne. And also lyenges ere forboden in þis commandement, and forswerrynge. Bot all lyenges are noghte dedly syn, bot if þay noye till som man bodyly or gastely.

¶ ix. The ninth (part of tenth) Commandment. Our neighbour's goods not to be wrongly coveted.

The nynde commandement es, 'Thow salt noghte couayte þe hous or oþer thynge mobill or in-mobill of þi neghtbour with wrange,' ne þou sall noghte hald oþer mens gude if þou may ȝelde thaym, elles þi penance saues þe noghte.

¶ x. The tenth (part) Commandment. We ought to love our neighbour as ourselves.

The tend commandement es, 'Thow salt noghte couayte þi neghtebour wyefe, ne his seruande, ne his mayden, ne mobylls of his.' He lufes God þat kepis thire commandementes for lufe. His neghtebour hym awe to lufe als hym selfe, þat es, till þe same gude þat he lufes hym-selfe to, na thynge till ill; and þat he lufe his neghtbour saule mare þan his body, or any gudeȝ of þe worlde, & cetera. Explicit.

VIII.

Item, Idem de septem donis Spiritus Sancti.
Also of the gyftes of the Haly Gaste. [On lf. 196.]

Þe seueñ gyftes of þe Haly Gaste þat ere gyfeñ to men and wymmeñ þat er ordaynede to þe Ioye of heueñ, and ledys thaire lyfe in this worlde reghtwysely:—Thire are thay, Wysdom̃, Vndyrstandynge, Counsayle, Strenghe, Connynge, Pete, The drede of God. Begynñ we at Consaile, for þare-of es myster at the begynnynge of oure werkes, þat vs myslyke noghte aftyrwarde. With thire seueñ gyftes þe Haly Gaste teches sere meñ screly. ¶ Consaile es doynge awaye of worldes reches, and of all delytes of all thynge3 þat mane may be tagyld with in thoghte or dede, and þat withdrawynge intill contemplacyone of Gode. ¶ Vndyrstandynge es to knawe whate es to doo and whate es to lefe, and þat that sall be gyffeñ, to gyffe it to thaym þat has nede, noghte till oþer þat has na myster. ¶ Wysedome es forgetynge of erthely thynges, and thynkynge of heuen, with discrecyone of all meñ dedys. In þis gyfte schynes contemplacyone, þat es, Saynt Austyñ says, A gastely dede of fleschely Affeccyones thurghe þe Ioye of Araysede thoghte. † ¶ Strenghe es lastynge to fullfill gude purpose, þat it be noghte lefte for wele ne for waa. ¶ Pete es, þat a man be mylde, and gaynesay noghte haly writte wheñ it smyttes his synnys, whethire he vndyrstand it or noghte, Bot in all his myghte purge he þe vilte of syñ in hym̃ and oþer. ¶ Connynge es, þat makes a man of gude, noghte ruysand hym̃ of his reghtewysnes, bot sorowand of his synnys, and þat man gedyrs erthely gude anely to the honour of God, and prow to oþer meñ þañ hym-selfe. ¶ The drede of God es, þat we turne noghte Agayne till oure syñ thurghe any ill eggyng. And þat es drede perfite in vs, and gastely, When we drede to wrethe God in þe leste syñ þat we kañ knawe, and flese it als venym̃. **Explicit.**

The seven gifts of the Holy Ghost.

I. Counsel, which is the taking up the contemplative life.

ij. Understanding, which teaches us how to distribute to the needy.

iij. Wisdom, which makes us think of Heaven. Austyn.

[† Lf. 196 bk.] iiij. Strength, which is stedfastness in good purpose.
v. Pity, which makes a man humble to receive the teaching of Holy Writ.
vj. Cunning, which makes a man penitent and charitable.
vij. The fear of God, which makes us fear to sin.

IX.

Item, idem de dilectacione in Deo.
Also of þe same,
delyte and ȝernyng of Gode.

Ihesus, Marie filius, sit michi clemens & propecius! Amen! 4

What delight in God is.

Gernyng and delite of Ihesu Criste, þat has na thyng of worldes thoghtes, es wondyrfull pure, haly, and faste; and when a man felis hym in þat degre, than es a man Circumsysede gastely. When all oþer besynes and affeccyons 8 and thoghtes are drawen away owte of his saule That he may hafe ryste in Goddes lufe, with-owtten tagillynge of oþer thynges.

Its wonderful power.

¶ The delyte es wondirfull. It es sa heghe þat na thoghte may reche þar-to to bryng it doun. ¶ It es pure, when it es noghte 12 blendid with na thynge þat es contrayrie thare-to. ¶ And it es

Three things which increase delight in God.

faste, when it es clene and stabill, delitande by it-selfe. ¶ Thre thynges makes delite in Gode heghe. Ane es, restreynynge of fleschely luste in compleccionne. Anoþer es, restreynynge or 16 repressynge of ill styrrynge and of temptacione in will. The thirde es, kepynge or hegheynge of þe herte in lyghtenynge of þe Halygaste, þat haldis his herte vpe fra all erthely thoghtes, þat he sette nane obstakill at the comynge of Criste in-till hym. 20 ¶ Ilkane þat couaytes endles hele, Be he besy nyghte and daye to fulfill þis lare, or elles to Cristeȝ lufe he may noghte wynn; For it es heghe, and all þat it duellis in, it lyftes abown layery lustes and vile couaytes, and abown all affeccyouns and thoghtes of 24

Two things which make this delight pure.

any bodily thynge. Twa thynges makes oure delyte pure. Ane es, ternynge of sensualite to the skyll. For, when any es tornede to delite of hys fyve wittes, alsonne vnclennes entyrs in-to his saule. Anoþer es, þat þe skyll mekely be vssede in gastely 28 thynges, als in medytacyons, and orysouns, and lukynge in haly bukes. For-thy þe delyte þat has noghte of vnordaynde styrrynge, and mekely has styrrynge in Criste, and in whilke þe sensualyte es tournede to þe skyll, all sette and eysede tyll 32 God, makys a mans saule in ryste & sekirnes, and ay to duell in

X. The union of God with the Soul of Man.

gude hope, & to be payede with all Godis sandes with-owtten gruchynge or heuynese of thoghte3, & cetera. **Explicit.**
Explicit carmen. Qui scripsit, sit benedictus! Amen!
† ¶ Incipit Speculum Sancti Edmundi Cantuarensis [† Leaf 197.]
Archipiscopi in Anglicis.
Here begynnys The Myrrour of Seynt Edmonde þe Ersebechope of Canterberye. [*Not printed here.*]

X.

[The Anehede of Godd with mannis saule.][1] [On lf. 219 bk.]

Dere Frende, wit þou wele þat þe ende and þe soueraynte of perfeccione standes in a verray anehede of Godd and of manes saule by perfyte charyte. This Ende þan es verrayly made, whene þe myghtes of þe saule er refourmede by grace to þe dignyte and þe state of þe firste condicione, þat es, whene þe mynde es stablede sadely, with-owtten † changynge and vagacyone, in Godd and gastely thynges, and when the resone es cleryde fra all worldly & fleschely behaldynges and Imagycyones, fygours and fantasyes of creatures, and es illumenede with grace for to be-halde Godde and gastely thynges, and when þe will and þe affeccyon es puryfiede and clensede fra all fleschely lustes, kyndely and werldly lufe, and es enflawmede with brennande lufe of þe Haly Gaste. Bot þis wondirfull anehede may noghte be fulfillede perfytely, contenually, ne hally in þis lyfe, for corrupcyon of þe flesche, Bot anely in þe blysse of heuen. Neuer-þe-lattere, þe nerre þat a saule in þis presente lyfe may come to þis anehede, þe mare perfite it es, For [þe mare] þat it es refourmede by grace till þe ymage and þe lyknes of his creatoure here one þis manere wyse, þe more Ioy and blysse sall it hafe in heuen. Oure Lorde Godd es ane Endles beynge with-owtten chaungynge, All-myghtty with-owtten faylynge, Souerayne wysdome, lyghte, sofastenes with-owtten errour or myrknes; Souerayne gudnes, lufe, Pees

The Union of God with man's Soul is the highest perfection.

[† Lf. 220.]

This Union may not be fully reached in this life.

The nature of God.

The nearer a soul can be

---
[1] This treatise, which is without heading in the MS., was ascribed to Richard Rolle by Sir F. Madden when he examined the Thornton MS. in 1835.

X. The blessings of the union of God with the Soul of Man.

brought to this nature the higher its advance.

and swetnes; þan, þe mare þat a saule es Anehede, festened, confo*ur*mede & Ioynede to oure Lorde Godd, þe mare stabiłł it es & myghty, þe mare wysse & clere, Gude, peyseble, luffande, and mare vertuous; and so it es mare perfite. For a saule þat haues, by grace of Ihesu, and lange trauayle of bodyly & gastely excercyse, ou*er*commeñ and dystroyede concupyscens and passiou*n*s, and vnskiłłwyse styrrynges wi*th*-in it-selfe, and wi*th*-owtteñ in þe sensualite, and es clede¹ in vertus,—as in mekenes and myldnes, in pacyence, in sothefastnes, in gastely strenghe and ryghtewisenes, in co*n*tynence, in wysdoñ, in trouthe, hope, and charyte,—þan es it made p*er*fite als it may be in þis lyfe. Mekiłł

The comfort a soul thus gains.

comforthe it reschayues of our*e* Lorde, no3te anely inwardly in his preue substance, be þe vertu of þe anehede to oure Lorde, þat lyes in knaweynge and lufynge of Godd, in lyghte of gastely bry*n*nynge of hyñ, in transfo*ur*mynge of þe saule in þe Godhede, Bot also in many oþ*er* comforthes, & Sauo*ur*s, swettnes, and wondirfułł felynges one sere maners. Aftir our*e* Lorde vouches safe to vesete his creato*ur*s here in erthe, and eftyre þe saule pro-fytes and waxes in charyte, Some saule (by vertue of charyte þat Godd gyffes it) es so clensede, þat ałł creaturs, in ałł þat he heris or sese, or felis by any of his wittes, turnes hyñ tiłł co*m*forthe and gladnes; and þe sensualite receyues newe savo*ur* and swetnes in ałł creaturs. And righte als before, þe lykynges in þe sensualite ware fleschely, vayne, and vecyous, for þe payne of þe orygynałłe syñ, righte so nowe þay ere made gastely, and clene, wi*th*-owtteñ

The fleshly nature made to minister to its delight.

bitt*er*nes and bytynge of co*n*cyence. And þis es þe gudnes of our*e* Lorde, þat, sen þe saule es puneschede in the sensualite, and þe flesche es p*ar*tynere of þe payne, That eftirwarde þe saule be comforthede in hir sensualite, and þe flesche be felawe of þe Ioye and comforthe wit*h* þe saule, noghte fleschely, bot gastely, als he

For this the dignity of the soul is shown. [† Lf. 220 bk.]

was felawe in tribulacione and payne. þis es þe fredom & þe lordchipe, † dygnyte and þe wyrchip*e*, þat a manes saule hase ou*er* ałł creaturs; The whylke dygnyte he may receyue by grace here, þat ilk a creature sauour*e* to hyñ als it es, and þat es, when by grace he sese, or he heres, or he felys anely Godd in ałł creaturs.

4

8

12

16

20

24

28

32

¹ *Stain in MS.*

X. *The Soul is made to hear the Song of Angels.* 17

One þis maner wyse a saule es made gastely in þe sensualite by abowndance of charite þat es in þe substance of the saule. Also oure Lorde comforthes a saule by Aungells sange. Bot what þat
4 sange es, it may noghte [be] dyscryuede be no bodyly lyknes, for it es gastely, and abown all manere of ymagynacyone and mans reson. It may be perceyuede and felide in a saule, bot it may noghte be spoken. Neuer-þe-lattere, I speke þare-of to þe als
8 me thynke. When a saule es puryfyede by þe lufe of Godd, Illumynede by wysedom, stabled by myghte of Godd, Than es þe eghe of þe saule opyned to be-halde gastely thynges, as vertus, Aungells, and haly saules, and heuenly thynges. Thane es þe saule
12 abill, by cause of clennes, to fele þe toucheynge, þe spekynge of gude Aungells. This touchyng and spekynge es gastely, noghte bodyly: For when þe saule es lyftede and raysede owte of the sensualyte, and owte of mynde of any erthely thynges, Than in
16 gret feruoure of lufe and lyghte of Godd, if oure Lorde vouche-safe, þe saule may here & fele heuenly sowun, made by þe presence of Aungells in louynge of Godd. Noghte þat þis sange of Aungells es souerayne Ioy of þe saule, Bot a defference þat es
20 by-twyxe a manes saule in flesche and ane Aungelle, be-cause of vnclennes. A saule may noghte here it, bot by rauyschynge in lufe, and nedis for to be puryfiede full clene, and fullfillide of mekyll charyte, are it ware abyll for to here heuenly sowun.
24 For þe souerayne and þe Escencyalle Ioy es in þe lufe of Godd by hym-selfe and for hym-selfe, and þe secundarye es in comonynge and byhaldynge of Aungells and gastely creaturs. For, ryghte as a saule, in vndirstandynge of gastely thynges, es of ofte sythes
28 touched and kennede thurghe bodyly ymagynacyone, by wyrkynge of Aungells (as Eʒechielle þe profete sawe in bodily ymagynacyonne þe sothefastnes of Goddes preuates), Righte so, in þe lufe of Godd, a saule, be þe presence of Aungelles, es raueschede owte
32 of all mynde of erthely and fleschely thynges in-to a heuenly Ioye, to here Aungells saunge and heuenly sowun, eftir þat þe charite es mare or lesse. Nowe than, thynke me, þat per may no saule fele verreyly Aungells sange ne heuenly sown, bot it be in perfite
36 charite. And noghte for-thi all þat are in perfite charyte no

Also our Lord comforts a soul by angels' song.

This cannot be fully described, but I will speak of it as I think.

The way to hear it is by an excess of love.

X. Danger of Mistakes in this Matter.

And not all those who are in perfect charity can hear it.

hase noghte felyde it, Bot anely þat saule þat es purede in þe fyre of lufe of Godd, þat alł erthely sauoure es brynte owte of it, and alł menes lettande be-twyx þe saule and þe clennes of Angells es broken and put awaye fra it. Þan sothely may he synge a newe sange, and sothely may he here a blysfulł heuenly sown

Our Lord knows the soul that for burning love is worthy to hear angels' song.
[† Lf. 221.]

and Aungells sange, with-owtten dessayte or feynynge. Oure Lorde wate whare þat saule es þat, for abowndance of brynnande lufe, es worthi to here Aungells sange. Wha-so þan wilł here Aungells sange, and noghte be dyssayuede by feynynge, † ne by ymagynacyone of hym-selfe, ne by illusyone of þe Enemy, hym behoues hafe perfite charite, and þat es, when alł vayne lufe and drede, vayne Ioy and sorowe, es casten owte of þe heite, þat he lufes na thynge bot Gcdd, ne dredis na thynge bot Godd, ne Ioyes ne sorowes na thynge bot in Godd, or of Godd. Who-so myghte, by þe grace of Godd, go þis way, he sulde noghte erre.

Some are deceived by their own imagination in this matter.

Neuer-þe-lattere som men ere disceyued by þaire awenn ymagynacyon, or by illucyon of þe Enemy in þis matere. Som man, when he hase lange trauelde bodily and gastely in dystroynge of synnes and getynge of vertus, and perauenture hase getyn by grace a tomdele ryste, and a clerete in concyence, onone he leues prayers, redyngs of haly writte, and medytacions of þe passione of Criste, and þe mynde of his wrechidnes, and, are he be callede of Godd, he gedyrs his wittys by violence to seke and to be-halde heuenly thynges, are his eghe be made gastely by grace, and ouertrauells by ymagynacionns his wittes, and by vndiscrete trauellynge turnes þe braynes in his heuedè, and forbrekes þe myghtes and þe wittes of þe saule and of þe body ; and

And are under delusions arising from physical causes.

þan, for febilnes of þe brayne, hym thynkes þat he heres woundirfulł sownes and sanges, and þat es no thynge ells bot a fantasie caused of trubblyng of þe brayne, as a man þat es in a frensye, hym thynkes þat he herys or sese þat na noþer man duse, and alł es bot vanyte and fantasie of þe heued ; or elles by wyrkyng of þe enemy þat fenys swylke sowune in h[is her]ynge. For if a man

This is the craft of the Devil.

hase any presumpcione in his fantasies and in his wirkynge, and þare-be falles in-to vndiscrete ymagynacyone, as it ware a frensye, and es noghte kennede ne rewlede of grace, ne comforthede by

X. *Danger of Mistakes in this Matter.*

gastely strenghe, þe deuelle entirs þan by fals illumynacyons, and fals sownnes and swetnes, and dyssaues a mans saule. And of þis false grounde spiynges errours and herysyes, false prophesyes, presumpcyons and false rusynngs, Blasfemyes, and sclandiiynges, and many oþer meschefes. And þare-fore, if ȝou se any man gastely ocupiede Falle in any of þise synnes, and þise dissaytes, or in frensyes, wit ȝou wele þat he herde neuer ne felide Aungells sange, ne heuenly sowne. For sothely, he þat verreyly heres Aungels sange, he es made so wyse ȝat he sall neuer erre by fantasye, ne by indiscrecyon, ne by no sleghte of þe deuelle. Also som men felis in theire hertes as it ware a gastely sowne and swete sanges of dyuerse maners, and þis es commonly gude, and somtyme it may turne tyll dissayte. Þis sowne es felide one þis wyse. Some man settis þe thoghte of his herte anely in þe name of Ihesu, and stedfastly haldis it þare-too; and in schorte tym hym thynkes that þat name turnes hym till gret comforthe and swetnes, and hym thynkes þat þe name sowunes in his herte delitably, as it were a saunge, and þe vertu of þis likynge es so myghty, þat it drawes in all þe wittes of þe saule þare-to. Who-so may fele þis sownne and þis swetnes verrayly in his herte, wite he wiele þat it es of Godd; and als lange als he es meke, he sall noghte be dissayuede. Bot þis es noghte Aungels sange, bot it es a saunge of þe saule, be vertu of þe name, and by touchynge of þe gude Aungels. For when a saule † offers it to Ihesu trewly & mekely, puttande all his traiste and his desyre in hym, and besily kepis in his mynde, Oure Lorde Ihesu, whene he will, puris þe affeccione of þe saule, and fillis it & fedis it with swetnes of hym-selfe, and makes his name in þe felynge of þe saule as hony, and as sange, and as any thynge þat es delitabill. So þat it lykes þe saule euer mare for to cry 'Ihesu, Ihesu'; and noghte anely he hase comforthe in þis, bot also in psalmes[1] and ympnes, and antymms of Haly Kyrke, þat þe herte synges þam swetely, deuotly, and frely, with-owtten any trauelle of þe saule, or bitternes, in þe same tym, and noteȝ þat Haly Kyrke vses. This es þe gude and of þe gyfte of Godd. For þe substance of þis

And no true hearing of angels' song.

Other delusions that may arise in the mind.

Danger arising from an intense devotion to the name of Jesus.

Difference between angels' song and the songs of the Lord.
[† Lf. 221 bk.]

---

[1] MS. spalmes.

X. Danger of Mistakes in this Matter.

Danger from vain-glory.

felynge lyes in þe lufe of Ihesu, whilke es fedde and lyghtenede by swilke maner of sanges. Neuer-þe-lattere, in þis maner felynge a saule may be disceyuede by vayne glorye, noghte in þat tyṁ þat þe affeccioñ synges to Ihesu and loues Ihesu in swetnes of hym, bot eftyrwarde, whan it cesses, & þe herte kelis of loue of Ihesu, Thañ entyrs in vayne glorie. Also sum mañ es dessayuede on þis wyese. He heris wele say þat it es gude to haue Ihesu in his mynde, or any oþer gude worde of Godd͗, and þañ he streynes his herte myghtyly to þat name, and by acostoṁ he hase it nerehande alway in his mynde. Noghte for-thi he felis nouþer þare-by, in his affeccyonne, swetnes, ne lighte of knawynge in his resouñ, bot anely a nakede mynde of Godd͗ or of Ihesu, or of Mary, or of any oþer gude worde. Here may be disceyte, noghte for it es ill to hafe Ihesu in mynde oñ þis wyse, Bot if he [think a thinge] and this mynde, þat es anely his aweñ wyrkynge by custoṁ, halde it a specyalle vesytacyoñ of oure Lorde, and thynke it mare þañ it es. For, wite þou wele, þat a nakede mynde or a nakede ymagycioñ of Ihesu or of any gastely thynge, with-owtteñ swetnes of lufe in þe affeccioñ, or with-owtteñ lyghte of knawynge in resouñ, es bot a blyndnes, and a waye to dessayte, if a mañ halde it in his aweñ mare þañ it es. Thare-fore I halde it sekyre þat he be meke in his aweñ felynge, and halde þis mynde in regarde noghte, till he mowe, be custoṁ and vsynge of þis mynde, fele þe fyre of lufe in his affeccioñ, and þe lyghte of knawynge in his resoñ. Loo! I haue tolde þe in þis mater a lyttill as me thynke; noghte affermande þat þis suffisches, ne þat þis es þe sothefastnes in þis mater. Bot if þe thynke it oþer-wyse, or elles any oþer mañ sauour by grace þe contrarye here-to, I leue þe sayinꝫ, and gyfe stede to hym. It sufficeth to me for to lyffe in trouthe princypally, and noghte in felynge.

Danger from a mere mechanical remembrance of the name of Jesus.

This is nothing but blindness and folly.

Our safety lies in humility.

These are my views, though others may be able to say more.

[*Follows, on Lf. 222, a Poem*: 32

þi Ioy be ilke a dele to serue thi Godd͗ to paye . . .

ends: Thow salt hym se with eghe
And come to Criste thi frende.]

Explicit, &c. 36

XI.

[ACTIVE AND CONTEMPLATIVE LIFE[1].]

†[b Rethirne and susteryne bodely and goostely, two maner of states ther bene in holy chirch, be the which cristen soules plesyñ God and gettyn hem the blisse of heveñ, the one is bodily, and the other is gostely. Bodely wirkynge longith principally to worldely men or women, the which haunteñ leuefully worldely goodes, and wilfully vsen worldely besynessis. Also itt longith to all yonge begynnynge men, which come newe oute of worldely synnes to the seruyce of God, forto make hem able to goostely wyrkynges, and forto breke downe the vnbuxomnes of the body be skill, And swich bodely wyrkynges that itt myght be souple and redy, and not moch contrarious to the spirite in gostely wyrkynge. For, as seynt Poule seith, as women was maade for man, and not man for womeñ, Ryght so bodely wirkyngis was maade for goostely, and not gostely for bodely. Bodely wirkyngis goth before, and gostely comyth aftir, so seith seynt Poule,

Non quod prius spirituale, sed quod prius animale, deinde spirituale.

[† Lf. 59.]
The two states in Holy Church, bodily and ghostly.

[Bibl. Reg. 17. C. xviii.]

The Ghostly state the highest.

---

[1] The Lincoln manuscript of this treatise being imperfect, the beginning, to p. 27, line 29, is supplied from a British Museum MS. (Bibl. Reg. 17. C. xviii). This, as will be observed, is in a different dialect from the Thornton MS., being more modern, and according to Mr. Morris's test of the verbal plurals, of Midland dialect. There is also a MS. of the treatise in Cambridge University Library, which differs in dialect from both the above, and appears to be of still later date. We give a sentence from each by way of comparison of the spelling:—

THORNTON.	B. M.	CAMBRIDGE.
meñ þat ware in prelacye and oþer also þat ware haly temperalle meñ had full charite in affeccione with-in and also in wirkynge with-owtteñ.	men that were in prelaci and othir also that were holy tempereli meñ had full cherite with affeccion with-in and also in wirkynge with-outeñ.	men þat wern in prelacie and oþere also þat wern temporal men hadde ful charite in affectioun withinne and also in werkynge with-outen.

XI. *The Works of the Active Life must go first.*

Bibl. Reg. . C. xviii.]
The Ghostly state not easily reached.

g Ostely werke comyth not firste; but firste comyth bodely werke that is doone by the body, and sithen comyth gostely aftir; and this is the cause why itt behouyth the to be soo, for we are borne in synne and in corrupcion of the flessh, by the which we be so blyndet and so ouerlaide, that we haue nethir the gostely knowynge of God by light of vndirstondynge, ne gostely felynge of hym by clene desire of lovynge. And for-thi we mowe not sodenly stir oute of this mirke pitte of this flesshly

[† Lf. 59 bk.] corrupcion into that gostely light. For we may not suffre † itt ne bere itt for sekenes of oure silfe, no more than we may with oure bodely¹ eene, when þei be sore, beholde the light of the sonne.

We must wait and work.
And therfor we muste abide, and wirke be processe of tyme.

F irste bi bodily werkis besili, vnto we be discharged of this hevy birthen of synne, þe which lettith vs fro goostely wirkynge, And till oure soule be somwhat clensid from gret

What bodily working is.
outewarde synnes, and abiled to gostely werke. By this bodely wirkynge that I spake of, may þou vndirstonde all maner of goode werke that thi soule doth by þe wittes and the membres of thi bodi vnto thi silfe,—as in fastynge, wakeynge, and in refreynynge of thi flesshly lustis, be othir pennaunce doynge,—or to thine even cristen, by fulfillynge of the dedis of mercy bodili or gostely, or vnto God, by suffrynge of all maner bodely mischeves

These works are pleasing to God.
for the loue of rightwisnes. And thees werkis doone in trouth by charite pleysyn God, with-out the which þei be noght. Than who-so desirith forto be occupied gostely, hit is sekir and profitable to hym that he be firste well assaide a longe tyme in this bodely ¹ wirkynge, for thies bodely dedis ar tokyne and shewynge of moralle vertues, with-oute which a soule is not

And a necessary foundation for spiritual advancement.
able forto werke gostely. Breke downe firste pride in bodely berynge, and also with-in thi herte, thynkynge, boostynge, and prikkynge and preysynge of thi silfe and of thi dedis, presumynge of thi silfe, and veynlikynge of thi silfe, of eny thynge that God hath sent the, bodili or gostely. Breke downe also envy and Ire ayene thyne even cristen, wheþer he be riche or pore, goode or ² badde, that þou hate hym nott, ne haue

---

¹ MS. bedely.   ² MS. of.

XI. *From them you may Advance to Spiritual Works.*

disdeyne of hym wilfully, † nethir in worde, ne in dede. Aɫso [† Lf. 60.]
breke doune Couatise or worldely goode, þat þou (for holdynge [Bibl. Reg. 17. C. xviii.]
or getynge or sauynge of itt) offende not thi conscience, ne breke
not charite to God and to thi even cristen, for loue of no
worldely gode, but that þou getiste to kepe itt and to spened
itt with-oute loue or vaynlikynge of itt, as reson askith, in
worship of God, and helpe of thyne evyn cristyn. Breke *When well exercised in bodily good works you may advance to spiritual works.*
doune also, as þou may, flesshely likynges, oþer in accidie or in
bodili ease, or glotonie, or licherye; and þan, whan þou haste be
weɫ trauailed and wele assaide in aɫ swich bodily werkes,
than may þou bi grace ordeyne the to goostely wirkynges.
Grace and the goodenes of oure lorde Ihesu Criste that he
hath shewed to the,—in with-drawynge of thyne herte fro luste
and from likynges of worldely vanite, and vse of flesshly synnes
and in the turnynge of thi wiɫ enterely to his seruyce and his
plesaunce,—bryngith into my herte much mater to loue hym in
his mercy. And also itt sterith me gretly to strength the in thi
goode purpos and thi wirkynge that þou haste begon, forto
brynge itt to a goode ende, if that I coude, and principally for
God, and sithen for tendir affeccion of loue which þou haste to
me, Thoffe I be a wrech and vnworthi. I knowe weɫ the
desire of thi herte, that þou desiriste gretely to serue oure Lorde
by goostely occupacion, and holy, with-oute lettynge or strobillynge of worldely besynes, þat þou myght com by grace to more
knowynge and gostely felynge of God, and of gostely thyngis.
This desire is goode, as I hope, and of God, for itt is sente vnto *The desire of the purely contemplative life good.*
† hym specially. Neuirtheles itt is to refreyne and rewlen by
discrecion, as even outwarde wirkynge aftir the state that þou [† Lf. 60 bk.]
arte in, for charite vnrewled turnyth som tyme into vice. And
for this is seid in holy write, 'Ordinauit in me caritatem,'
That is to sey, oure Lorde yevYnge to me cherite, sett itt in ordir, *But even the best things not always right.*
and in reule, that itt shulde nat be loste by myne discrecion.
Right so this charite and this desire that oure Lorde hattth
yeven, of his mercy, to the, is forto rule and ordeyne how thou
shalte pursewe itt, aftir þi degre askith, and aftir the lyvynge
that thou haste vsed by-for this tyme, and after the grace of

XI. The Union of the two Lives.

vertues that þou now haste. Thow shalt not vttirly folow thi desire forto leve occupacion and besynes of the worlde which ar nedefull to vsen, iñ reulynge of thi silfe and of all othir that ar vndir thi kepynge, and yeve the holy to gostely occupacion of prayers and holy meditacions as itt were a frere or a monke, or anoþer mañ that war not bondeñ to the worlde by children and seruantes as þou arte, for itt fallith not to the. And if þou doo soo, thou kepiste not the ordire and charite. Also yf þou woldiste leveñ vttirly gostely occupacion, namely now aftir þe grace that God hath yeveñ vnto þe, and sett the holy to the besynes of the worlde, to the fulfillynge of the werkis of actife liffe as fully as anothir mañ that nevir felt deuocioñ, thou leuyste the ordir of cherite, for thi state askith forto doo both ilkoñ of hem in dyvyrs tymes. Thou shalt medle the werkes of acttife liffe with goostely werkes of live comtemplatyfe, and than þou doste wele. For þou shalt oo tyme with Martha be besy forto reule and gouerne thi householde, thi children, thi seruantes, þi neghboris, and thi tenantes; if þei do well, comforth hem there-in and helpe hem; if thei do evill, forto teche hem, amende hem, and chastise hem. And thou shalt also loke and knowe wysely thi thyngis and thi worldely goodes, þat þei be ryghtwysly kepte bi thi seruantes, gouerned and truly spendid, that þou myght the more plentivosly fulfill the dedis of mercy with hem vnto thyne evyn cristen. Also thou shalt, with Maria, leve besines of the world, and sitt dovne at the fete of oure Lorde by mekenes in prayers, and in holy thoghtes and in contemplacioñ of hym as he yevith the grace; and so shalt þou goo from the oone to the othir medefully, and fulfill hem both, and than kepiste þou well the ordir of cherite.

Vnto what maner of men longith actiffe liffe.

n euertheles, that þou haue no wondre of this that I say, þerefore I shall tell and declare to the a litill of this more opynly. þou shalt vnderstonde that þere is iij maner of livyngis: One is actife, anothir comtemplatife, the thride is made of both, and that is medlid. Actyfe liffe alon, that longith to worldely

XI. Those to whom each Separately Appertains.

men and women which ar lerned in knowynge¹ of gostely [Bibl. Reg. 17. C. xviii.]
occupacion, for þei fele no sauoure ne deuocion be feruo*ur* of loue, Those who are called to the Active life.
as othir men doo, ne thei can no skiłł of itt, and yitt nevirtheles
4 thei haue drede of God, and of the payne of hełł, and þerefore thei
† fle synne, and thei haue desire forto please God, and forto com [† Lf. 61 bk.]
to heven, and a goode wille hauen to her even͂ cristen͂. Vnto
these men itt is nedefułł and spedefułł to vse the werkis of Actife
8 liffe als besili as þei may, in the helpe of hem silfe and of hir
even cristen͂, for thei can nott els doo.

Vnto which men longith contemplatife liff.

C ontemplatife liffe alon longith to swyche men and women Those who are called to the life Contemplative.
12 that, for the loue of Godd, for-saken ałł opyn synnes of the
worlde, and of hir flessh̄, and ałł besynes chargis, and grevance
of worldely goodis, and maken hem silfe pore and naked, to the
bare nede of the bodili kynde, and fre fro soue*raynte of alle
16 othir men, to the s*eruice of God. Vnto thies men itt longith
forto trauaile and occupy hem inwardly forto gett, thorow the
grace of our Lorde, clennes in herte, and pes in conscience, bi the
distroynge of synne and receyvynge of vertues, and so forto com
20 to the comtemplacion͂; which clennes may not be hådd˙ with-out
gret excersyice of body and continuełł trauaile of the spirit, in
deuoute prayers, feruent desires, and gostely meditacions.

Vnto which men longith medelid liffe.

24 T he thride liffe, that is, medlid liffe, itt longith to men of Those who are called to the Mixed life.
holi-chirch, as to p*r*elates and to oþer Curatis, the which
han cure and soue*rante ouer othir men forto teche and reule hem, The secular clergy.
both hir bodies and hir soules, principally in͂ fulfillynge of the
28 dedis of mercy bodili and gostely. Vnto thes men itt longith
som tyme to vsen͂ werkis of mercy in actife liffe, in͂ helpe and
sustinaunce of hem silfe and of hir sugettis and of othir also,
† and som tyme forto leve ałł maner of besines ovtewarde, and [† Lf. 62.]
32 yeve hem vnto prayers and meditacions, and redynge of holy
writt, and to othir gosteli occupacions, after that thei fele hem

¹ nothing (?).

XI. To whom the Mixed Life Appertains.

[Bibl. Reg. 17. C. xviii.] Rich men who have devout inclinations.

disposed. Also itt longith to som temperall men, the which han soueraynte with michell haver of worldely goodis, and han also as itt wer lordisshipe ouer othir men forto gouerne and sustene hem, as a fader hath ovir his children, a maistre ouer his seruantis, and a lorde ovir his tenantes, the which men han also receyved of oure Lordes yifte grace of deuocion, and in party sauoure of gostely occupacion, vnto these men also longith medlid

Such men cannot abandon their active duties without sin.

liffe, that is both actife and contemplatife. For if þese men, stondynge the charge and the bonde which thei haue taken, wille leve vtterly the besynes of the world, the which owe skilfully to be vsed in fulfillynge of hir charge, and hooly yeve hem to contemplatife liffe, thei doo not well, for thei kepe nott the ordir of cherite. For charite, as þou knowiste, lith both in loue of God and of thyne evyn cristen, and þere-fore itt is resounable, that he that hath cherite, vse both, in wirkynge now to the one and now to the othir. For he þat, for the loue of God in contemplacion, levith the loue of his evyn cristen, and doth not to hym as

Neither must they neglect spiritual duties.

he oght when he is bonden þere-to, he fulfillith no cherite. Also, on the contrary wise, who-so hath¹ gret rewarde to wirke actife liffe and to besinnes of þe worlde that, for the loue of his evyn cristen, he levith gostely occupacion vtterly, after þat God hath disposed hem there-too, thei fulfill not cherite. This is the seynge

Our Lord practised the Mixed life.

of seynt Gregory. For-thi our Lorde, forto stere som forto vse this medlid liffe, toke vpon hym silfe the person of swiche

[† Lf. 6a bk.]

† maner of men, both of prelates, and of othir swich as ar disposed ther-to as I haue seide, and yave hem ensample, by his owen wirkynge, that thei shulde vse this medlid liffe as he did, that tyme he comyned with men and medled with men, shewynge to hem his dedis of mercy. For he taght the vn-couthe and vnkunnynge by his prechynge, he vesited þe seke, and helid hem of hir sores, he fedde the hungry, and he conforted the sory. And an othir tym he lefte þe conuersacion of all worldely men, and of his disciplis, and went into disserte vpon the hilles, and continued all night in prayers alone, as the gospell seith. Þis medlid liffe shewith oure Lorde in hym silfe to ensample of all

¹ MS. hatith.

XI. Holy Bishops have practised this Life.

othir that han taken the charge of þis medlid liffe, that þei shuld oo tyme yeveñ hem to besynes and worldely thyngis att resonable nede, and to the werkes of actiffe liffe in profitt of her encres-
4 ynge, which þei haue cure of. And añ othir tyme yive hem holy to deuocion and to contemplacion, in prayers and in meditacion.

[Bibl. Reg. 17. C. xviii.]

How holy bisshopes vsed medled liffe.

t his liffe ledde and vsed this holy Bisshopis be-for, which
8 had cure of mennes soules, and ministracion of temperaɫɫ goodes. For thes holy meñ lefte not witterly the ministracion of the lokynge and the dispendynge of worldely goodes, and yeve hem holy to comtemplacion, as moch comtemplacion as thei had.
12 But thei lefte fuɫɫ of hir owen reste in comtemplacion when[1] thei had weɫɫ lever haue bene stiɫɫ þat, for loue of hir even cristeñ, þei intermettid hem with worldely besynes in helpynge of hir sugettis; and sothly that was charite. For wysely and
16 discretely thei departed hir letvynge in two: O tyme thei fulfilled the lower party of cherite bi werkes of Actife liffe, for thei wer bonden þer-to by takynge of theire prelacies; And a-nothir tyme thei fulfilled the hyer party of cherite, iñ contemplacion
20 of God and of gostely thyngis, by prayers and meditacions; and so thei had cherite to God and to hir evyñ cristeñ, both in affeccion of soule with-iñ, And also with shewynge of bodili dedis with-outeñ. Oþer men that wer oonly contemplatiffe, and
24 were free from aɫɫ cures and prelaci, þei had fuɫɫ cherite to God and to hir evyñ cristen, but itt was oonly in affeccioñ of hir soule, and not iñ outewarde shewynge; and in hap so moch itt was more fuɫɫ inwarde, þei[2] myght not, ne itt nede not, ne itt
28 feɫɫ not for hym̄.

Holy bishops have used this life.

And in both parts of it exercised charity. [† Lf. 63.]

But these]† meñ þat were in prelacye, and oþer also þat were haly temperalle meñ, had fuɫɫ charite in affeccione with-in, and also in wirkynge with-owtteñ; and þat is propirly þis mellide
32 lyfe, þat es made bathe of actyffe lyfe and of contemplatyfe lyfe.

[† Thornton MS. leaf 223.]

And sothely for swilke a mañ þat es in spirituelle soueraynte, as in prelacye, in cure, in gouernance of oþer, as prelates bene,

The mixed life the best for prelates

---
[1] MS. whei.   [2] MS. þei þei.

XI. *The Religious Claims of the Mixed Life.*

And lords and those who have temporal possessions.

or in temperalle soueraynte, as werldly lordes and maysters bene, I halde þis mellide lyfe beste, and maste by-houely to þam̄, als lange als þay ere bowndeñ þer-to.

But for others the life contemplative the best.

Bot to oþer, þat ere fre, and noghte bowndeñ to temperale mynystracyoñ, ne to spiritualle, I hope þat lyfe contemplatyfe allane, if þay myghte com̄ sothefastly þare-to, were beste and maste spedfuƚƚ, maste medfuƚƚ and faire, and maste worthi to þam̄ for to vse and to halde, & noghte for to leue wilfully for nane owtwarde werkes of actyfe lyfe, Bot if it ware in gret nede, at gret releuynge & comforthynge of oþer meñ, ouþer of þaire body or of þaire saule.

Which however may be abandoned if need require.

Thañ, if nede aske, at þe prayere and instaunce of oþer, or elles at þe biddynge of oþer gouernaunce, I hope it es gude to þam̄ for to schewe owtwarde werkes of actyfe lyfe for a tym̄, in helpynge of þaire euencristeñ. By this that I hafe saide, þou may in party vndirstande whilke es a lyfe and whilke es oþer, and whilke accordis maste to thi state of lyffynge.

But for thee the mixed life is most fit as being placed in a post of dignity and rule.

And sothely, as me thynke, this Mellid lyfe accordis maste to þe; For, señ owre Lorde hase ordaynede þe and sett þe in þe state of soueraynte ouer oþer, als mekeƚƚ als it es, and lent þe habowndance of werldly gudes for to rewle and susteñ specyaly aƚƚ þose þat are vndire thi gouernance and thi lordchipe, after thi myghte & thi cunnynge, and also after thou hase ressayuede grace of þe mercy of oure Lorde Godd' for to hafe sumwhate knawynge of thi selfe, and gastely desyre and savour of his lufe, I hope þat þis lyfe þat es mellide es beste, and accordes maste to þe for to trauelle þe þare-in;

It is fitting that you should carefully divide your life into two parts, one for religion, one for business.

And þat es, to depart wyesly thi lyffynge in two; a tyme to þe tane, and anoþer tyme to þe toþer; For, wiet þou wele, if þou leue nedfuƚƚ besynes of actyf lyfe, and be rekles, and take na kepe of thi werldly gudes, how þay be spendide and kepide, ne hafe no force of thi sugetis and of thyñ euencristeñ, by-cause of desire and wiƚƚ þat þou hase anely for to gyffe þe to gastely ocupacyoñ, wenande þat þou arte therby excusede—if þou do so, þou dose noghte wysely. Whate are aƚƚ thi werkes worthe, whethire þay be bodyly or gastely, bot if thay be done ryghtefully and resonnably, to þe wirchipe of Godd', and at His byddynges? Now sothely, righte noghte. Thane, if þou leue þat thynge þat þou

XI. This is an Acceptable Service of Our Lord. 29

arte bowndeñ to, by way of charite, apoñ righte and resoñ, and wiłł hally gyffe þe to a-noþer thynge, wilfully as it ware, for mare plesance of hym, † whilke þou arte noghte bowndeñ to, Thou 4 dose noghte wirchipe discretly to Hym̄. Thou arte besy to wirchipe his heuede and his face, and aray it faire and curyusly, bot þou leues his body and þe armes and þe fete raggede and rente, and takes no kepe þare-of. And þan þou wirchipis hym̄ 8 noghte. For it es a velany, a mañ for to be curyously arrayede apoñ his heuede with perré and precyous stanes, and ałł his body be nakide and bare, as it ware a beggere. Righte so, gastely, it es no wyrchipe to Godd' for to couer His heuede and 12 leue His body bare. Thou sałł vndirstande, þat oure Lorde Ihesu Criste, as mañ, es heuede of a gastely body, whilke es Haly Kirke. The membris of this body are ałł cristeñ meñ. Som̄ are armes, and som̄ are fete, and som̄ ere oþer membris, 16 aftire sundre wirkynges þat þay vse in thaire lyffynge. Than, if þou be besy with ałł þi myghte for to arraye his heuede, þat es, for to wirchipe hym̄ selfe by mynde of his passioñ or of his oþer werkes in his manhede, by deuocyoñ and meditacioñ of Hym̄, 20 and forgetis His fete, þat ere thi childire, thi seruanteȝ, thi tenauntes, and ałł thyñ euencristyñ, and latis þam̄ spiłł for defaute of kepynge—vnarayede, vnkepide, and noghte tente to as þam̄ aughte for to be,—thow pleses Hym̄ noghte, For þou 24 duse no wirchipe to Hym̄. Thou makes þe for to kysse His mouthe by deuocyoñ and gastely prayere, bot þou tredis apoñ His fete and defoules þam̄, in als mekiłł als þou wiłł noghte tente to thaym̄ for neclygence of þi-selfe, of whilke þou hase takyñ 28 cure. ¶ Thus me thynke. ¶ Neuer-þe-lesse, if þou thynke þat þis es noghte sothe, for it ware a fayrere offyce to wyrchype þe heuede of Hym̄, as for to be alday ocupiede in meditacyoñ of His manhede, þan for to go lawere to oþer werkes, and make 32 clene his fete, as for to be besy bathe in thoghte and dede aboute þe helpe of thyñ euencristeñ in tyme,—Me thynke noghte so as vn-to þe. ¶ Sothely, He wiłł cuñ the more thanke for meke waschehynge of His fete wheñ thay ere righte foule and stynkyng 36 appoñ the, þan for ałł þe precyouse payntynge and þe arraynge

To devote yourself entirely to God, neglecting worldly duties, is not pleasing to Him.

[† Lf. 223 bk.]

This is to pay respect to the head but to neglect the lower members.

Christ is the head of a body, which is Holy Church.

And this His body must be your care or you will not please Him.

He will not thank you for devotion to Himself, if you neglect His poorer members.

XI. This is True Spiritual Occupation.

þat þou haue made aboute His heuede by mynde of His manhede. For it es faire enoghe, and nedis noghte mekiłł to be arrayede of þe. Bot His fete and His oþer membris, that ere thi sugetts and thyñ euencristyñ, ere sumtyme euyłł arrayede, and had nede for 4 to be lukede to and holpyñ by þe, & namely señ þou erte bowndeñ þare-to; and for thaym wiłł He cun the mekiłł thanke, if þou wiłł mekely and tendirly luke þam. For þe mare lawe seruyce þat þou duse to þi Lorde, for lufe of Hym̄, vn-to any of 8 His membris, wheñ nede and rightwysnes askes, with a glade meke herte, the mare pleseȝ þou Hym̄: thynkand þat it ware enoghe for þe for to be at þe leste degre & laweste state, sen it es His wiłł at it be so; For it semys, sen He hase putt þe in þat 12 state, for to trauelle and serue oþer meñ, þat it es His wiłł þat þou suld fulfiłł it at thi myghte. This ensample I say to þe, noghte for þou duse noghte þus as I say, For I hope þou duse þus and better, Bot for I walde þat þou sulde do þus † gladly, and 16 noghte for to leue sumtyme gastely ocupacyoñ, and entermete þe with werldly besynes, in wyse kepynge and dispendynge of thi werldly gudes, and gud rewlynge of þi seruauntes and þi tenauntes, and in oþer gude werkes doynge, vn-to ałł þinne 20 euencristeñ at þi myghte; Bot for þat þou sulde doo bathe in dyuers tym̄ with a gud wiłł, þe tane and þe toþer, if þou myghte; as if þou hade prayede and bene ocupiede gastely, þou sałł aftir certeyne tym̄ breke of þat, and þou sałł besyly and 24 gladly ocupye þe in sum̄ bodily ocupacioñ vnto thyne eueñ cristeñ. Also when þou hase bene besye owtwarde a while with thi seruauntes, or with oþer meñ profytably, þou sałł breke offe, and com̄ agayne to þi prayers and thi deuocyoñ, after Godd' 28 gyfs þe grace; and so sałł þou put away, by grace of oure Lorde, Sleuthe, ydilnes, and vayne riste of thi selfe, þat comes vndir coloure of contemplacioñ, and lettes þe sumtyme fra medfułł and spedfułł ocupacioñ in owtwarde besynes; and þou sałł be ay 32 wele ocupiede, ouþer bodyly or gastely. Thare-fore, if þou wiłł do wele, þou sałł gastely, als as Iacob did bodily. ¶ Haly Write saise þat Iacob, wheñ he begane for to serue his mayster Labane, he couete Rachelle, his mayster doghter, to his wyfe, for hir 36

XI. Lessons from the History of Jacob, Leah, and Rachel.

fairehede; and for hir he seruede. Bot wheñ he wende to hafe hade hire to his wife, he tuke firste Lya, þe toþer doghter, in stede of Rachelle; and aftirwarde he tuke Rachelle; and so he hade
4 bathe at þe laste. By Iacob in Haly Writt es vndirstande ane ouerganger of synnes. By þise two wymmeñ ere vndirstandeñ, as Sayne Gregor saise, two lyfes in Haly Kyrke, actyfe lyfe and contemplatyfe. Lya es als mekill at say as trauyliouse, and
8 betakyns actyfe lyfe. Rachelle, syghte of begynnynge, þat es, Godd, and betakyns lyfe contemplatyfe. Lya was frwtefull, bot scho was sare eghede. Rachelle was faire and lufely, bot scho was barrayne. Than, righte as Iacob couetid Rachelle for hir
12 fairehede, and neuer-þe-lesse he had hir noghte wheñ he walde, bot firste he tuke Lya and aftir-warde hir, Righte so, ilk mañ, turnede by grace of compunccyoñ sothefastly fra synnes of þe werlde and of þe flesche, vn-to þe seruyce of Godd, and clennes
16 of gude lyffynge, hase gret desyre and gret langynge for to hafe Rachelle, þat es, for to hafe ryste and gastely swetnes in deuocyoñ and contemplacioñ, for þat es so faire and so lufely. And in hope for to hafe þat lyfe anely, he disposes hym for to serue
20 oure Lorde wyth all his myghtes. Bot ofte wheñ he wenes for to hafe Rachelle, þat es, riste in deuocyoñ, Oure Lorde suffers hym firste for to be assayede wele and trauelde with Lya, þat es, ouþer with gret temptacions of þe werlde or of þe deuelle, or
24 ells with oþer werldly besynes, bodily or gastely, in helpyng of his euencristyñ. And wheñ he es wele trauelde with þam, and nerhande ouer-commeñ, Thañ oure Lorde gyffes hym Rachelle, þat es, grace of deuocyoñ, and riste in concience. And so hase
28 he bathe Rachelle and Lya. So sall þou do after ensaumple of Iacob, take þise two lyfes, actyfe † & contemplatyfe, sen Godd hase sett the bathe þe tane and þe toþer. By þe taa lyfe þat es actyfe, þou sall brynge furthe fruyte of many gude dedis in helpe
32 of thyñ euencristeñ; And by þe toþer, þou sall be made and bryghte and clene in þe behaldynge of souerayne bryghtnes, þat es Godd, begynnynge and ende of all þat es made. And þan sall þou be sothefastly Iacob, and ouerganger and ouercommere of all
36 synnes; and after, by þe grace of Godd thi nam sall be chaungede,

By Jacob is meant one who overcomes sins.

Leah and Rachel are the two sorts of lives, active and contemplative.

Those that desire Rachel are often first obliged to take Leah.

But afterwards Rachel is given.

You must take both the lives.
[†Lf. 224 bk.]

Thus shall you be like Jacob, an overcomer of sins, and then

XI. We should Rejoice in Performing the Duties of Active Life.

Israel, that is, one that sees God.
as Iacobe name was turnede in-to Israel. Israel es als mekill at say, als a man seande Godd. Than, if þou be firste Iacob, and discretly will vse þise two lyfes in tyme, þou sall be aftir Israel, þat es, verray contemplatyfe. Ouþer in þis lyfe he will delyuer 4 þe, and make þe free fra charge of besynes whilke þou ert bounden to, or ells after þis lyfe fully in þe blysse of Heuen when þou comes thedire. ¶ Contemplatyfe lyfe es faire and medfull, and þare-fore þou sall aye hafe it in desyre. Bot þou 8

You may desire the life contemplative, but you must use the life active.
sall hafe in vsesynge mekill þe lyfe actyfe, for it es so nedfull and so spedfull. And þare-fore if þou be putt fra thi reste by deuocyon when þe ware leueste be still þar-at, by thy childire, thy seruantes, or by any of thyn euencristen, for þaire profyte or 12

Therefore be not sad if worldly business takes you from your devotion, but do it as for Christ and it shall be spiritually profitable to you.
ese of þaire hertes skilfully askide, be noghte angry with þam, ne heuy, ne dredfull, as if Godd'wald be wrathe with the þat þou lefte Hym for any oþer thynge, For it es noghte so. Bot lyghtly þou leue of thi deuocyon, wheþer it be in prayers or in medi- 16 tacyons, and goo do thi dett and þi seruyse to þine euencristen als redily als if oure Lorde hymselfe bade þe do so. And suffire mekely for His lufe with-owtten gruchynge, if þou may, and dissese and trubblynge of þi herte by-cause of mellynge with 20 swylke besynes, For it may fall sumtyme þat þe trubylyere þat þou hase bene owtwarde with actyfe werkes, The mare brynnande desyre þou sall hafe to Godd, and þe more clere syghte of gostely thynges, by grace of owre Lorde, in deuocyon when þou comes 24 þare-to. For it faris þer-by as if þou hade a littill cole, and þou

The good works of active life are like the sticks which cause the coal to burn.
walde make a fyre þare-with, and ger it bryn. Thow wald fyrste lay to stykkes, and ouer-hille þe cole; and if it semyd as for a tym þat þou sulde qwenche þe cole with þi stykkes, Neuer-þe-lesse, 28 when þou hase habedyn a while, and after blawes a lyttill, Onane spryngez a grete flawme of fyre, for þe stykkes ere turnede to fyre. Righte so gastely, thi will and thi desyre þat þou hase to Godd, it es, as it ware, a littill cole of fyre in þi 32 saule, For it gyffes to þe sumwhate of gostely hete and gostely lyghte; bot it es full lyttill, For ofte it waxes colde, and turnes to fleschely riste, and sumtyme into ydilnes. For-þi it es gude þat þou putte þare-to stykkes, þat ere gud werkes of actyfe lyfe. 36

XI. Good Deeds a True Service of God.

And if so bee þat þire werkes, as it semes, for a tyṁ lette thi
desyre, þat it may noghte be so clene ne so feruente as þou walde,
Be noghte to dredfull þare-fore, Bot habyde and suffire a while,
4 and go blawe at þe fyre, þat es, firste do thi werkes, and go þaiñ *Fear not that*
allane to þi prayers and thi meditacyons, and lyfte vpe thi herte *God will not accept the*
to Godd, and pray Hym of His gudnes þat He will accepte thi *works done to please him.*
werkis þat þou duse to His plesance. Halde þou † þaṁ as noghte [† Lf. 225]
8 in thyne aweñ syghte, bot anely at þe mercy of Hyṁ. Be a-
knowe mekely thi wrechidnes and thi frelte, and arett all thi
gude dedis sothefastely to Hyṁ, in als mekill als þay ere gude;
and in als mekill als þay ere badde, noghte donne with all þe
12 circumstance þat ere nedfull vn-to gude dedis, for defaute of dis-
crecioñ, put thaṁ vn-to thi selfe. And for þis meknes sall all
thi dedis turne in-to flawme of fyre, as stykkes laide apoñ þe cole.
And so sall gude dedis owtewarde noghte hyndire thi deuocyoñ, *Your good*
16 bot raþer make it mare. Oure Lorde sayse in Haly Write þus: *deeds will not hinder your devotion, but*
¶ 'Ignis in altare meo semper ardebit, et sacerdos mane surgens *rather make it more.*
subiciet ligna, ut ignis non extynguatur.' 'Fyre,' he sayse, 'sall [Levit. vi. 12.]
bryñ in myne autir, and þe priste rysande at morne sall putt
20 vndire stykkys, þat it be noghte qwenchede.' This fire es lufe and
desire to Godd' in saule; whilke lufe nedis to be nureschede and
kepide by laynnge to of stykkis, þat it goo noghte owtte. Thise
stykkes ere of dyuerse matire: Soṁ ere of a tre, and soṁ er of
24 anoþer. A maiñ or a womañ þat es letterede, and hase vndir- *The fire of devotion*
standynge in Haly Writt, if he hafe þis desire of deuocyoñ in his *must be fed with divers*
herte, It es gude vn-to hyṁ for to gedire hyṁ stekkis of haly *sorts of fuel.*
ensaumpills and saynges of oure Lorde by redynge3 of Haly Write,
28 and noresche þe fyre with thayṁ. Anoþer mañ or a womañ *One is learn-ed in Holy*
vnletterede may noght so redyly hafe at his hand Haly Writt *Writ and doctors' saws.*
and doctours sawes, and for-thi it nedis to hym to do many gud *Another*
werkis owtewarde to his eueñ cristyñ, and kyndill þe fire of lufe *being unlet-tered must*
32 with thaṁ. And so it es gude, ilke mañ in his degre, aftir he es *be content with bodily*
disposede, þat he gette hym stykkes of a thyng or of oþer, ouþer *deeds.*
prayers or gude meditacyons, or redynges in Haly Writt, or gude
bodily wyrkynges, for to nuresche þe desire of lufe in his saule
36 þat it be noghte qwenchede; For þe affeccyoñ of lufe es tendir

R.H. D

and lyghtly wiłł vanysche awaye, bot if it be wele kepide, and by gud dedis bodyly or gastely contenualy nuresched.

As you have received a spark of this fire you must nourish it with fuel. [Deut. iv. 24.]

Now þan, señ oure Lorde hase sente in-to thi herte a littiłł sparke of his blysside fire, þat es hym̄-selfe, as Haly Writt saise 'Deus noster ignis consumens est,' 'oure Lorde es fyre wastande'—For as bodily fyre wastes ałł bodily thynges þat may be wastyde, Righte so gastely fyre, þat es Godd, wastis ałł maner of syñ whare-so it fallis; and for-thi oure Lorde es lykkende to fyre wastande. I pray þe

my dearsister. hertly, dere syster, noresche þis fire. This fire es noghte ełłis bot lufe and charyte; þis hase He sent in-tiłł erthe, as He saise

[Luc. xii. 49.] in the Gosepelle, 'Ignem veni mittere in terram, et ad quid nisi ut ardeat.' 'I am commeñ,' He saise, 'for to send fyre of lufe intiłł erthe, and whare-to þat it suld bryñ;' Þat es, Godd hase

This fire is the desire for God. sent fire of lufe, þat es, gude desyre and a grete wiłł vn-to plese Hym̄, in-to manes saule, and vn-to þis ende, þat a mañ suld

[† Lf. 225 bk.] knawe † it, kepe it, noresche it and strenghe it, and be sauede thare-by. The more desire þat þou hase vn-to Hym̄, þe more es this fyre of lufe in the. The lesse þat thi desire es, þe lesse es þis fire. The mesure of þis desyre, how mekiłł it es, noþer in thi selfe, ne in na noþer, knawes þou noghte, ne no mañ of hym-selfe, Bot Godd allone þat gyffes it; and for-thi dispuyte noghte with þi selfe as if þou wolde knawe how mekiłł thi desire es, Bot be besy for to desyre als mekiłł als þou may, Bot noghte for to wete þe mesure of thi desyre. Sayne Austyñ saise, þat þe lyfe of euer-ilk a gude Cristyñ mañ es a contenuelle desire to Godd, and þat es of a gret vertue, For it es a gret crying in þe erris of Godd; þe more þat þou desires, þe heghere þou cries; þe better þou prayes, þe wyseleere þou thynkis. And what es þis

And it consists in earnest longing for heavenly things and despising of this world. desire? Now, sothely, na thyng bot a lathynge of ałł þis werldis blysse, of ałł fleschely lykynges in thi herte, and a qwemfułł langynge, with a thristy 3ernyng, to heuenly Ioye and endles blysse. This, thynke me, may be callid a desire of Godd. If þou hafe þis desire, as I hope sekirly þat þou hase, I pray the kepe it wele, and noresche it wysely; and wheñ þou sałł pray or thynke, make þis desire begynnynge of ałł þi werke for to encresse it.

XI. The Blessings which it brings.

Luke after na noþer bedily swetnes, noþer sownyng ne sauourynge, ne wondirfull lyghte, ne Aungells syghte, ne if oure Lorde hym-selfe, as vn-to þi syghte, walde appere to þe bodily; charge it bot a lytill; Bot at all thi besynes be þat þou myghte fele sothefastly in thi thoghte a lathynge and a full forsakynge of all maner of syn and of vnclennes, with a gastely syghte of it, how foule, how vggly, and how paynfull þat it es; and at þou myght hafe a myghty desyrynge to vertus, to mekenes, to charite, and to the blysse of Heuen. This, thynke me, ware gastely comforthe and gastely swetnes in a mans saule, as for to hafe clennes in concience, fra wikkidnes of all werldly vanyte, with stabill trouthe, meke hope, and full desyre to Godd. *This must needs bring comfort and blessing to the soul.*

How-so-euer it es of oþer conforthes and swetnes, me thynke þat swetnes sekire and sothefaste þat es felid in clennes of concyence, by myghty forsakynge and lathyng of all syn, and by in-ward syghte, by feruent desyre of gastely thyngis. And oþer confortes or swetnes, or any oþer maner of felynges, bot if þay helpe and lede to þis ende, þat es, to clennes in conscience, and gastely desyre of Godd, ere noghte full sekire for to reste one. But now may þou aske wheþer this desyre be lufe of Godd. As vn-to þis I say, þat þis desire es noghte propirly lufe, bot it es a begynnynge; For lufe propirly es a full cuppillynge of þe lufande and þe lufed to-gedyre, as Godd and a saule, in-to ane. This cuppillyng may noghte be had fully in this lyfe, Bot anely in desyre and langynge þare-to; as if a man† lufe anoþer whilke es absent, he desyris gretly his presence, for to hafe þe vys of his lufe and his likyng. Righte so gostely, als lang als we erre in þis life, oure Lorde es absent fra vs, þat we may noþer se Hym, ne here Hym, ne fele Hym als He es, and þare-fore we may noghte hafe þe vis of His lufe here in fulfilling. Bot we may hafe a desyre and a gret ȝernynge for to be present to Hym, for to se Hym in His blysse, and to be anede to Hym in lufe. This desyre may we hafe of[1] His gyfte in þis life, by þe whilke we sall be safe, For it es lufe vn-to Hym as it may be hade here. This Sayne Paule saide, 'Scientes quidem *But this desire is not the full love of God, but only the beginning of it.* [† Lf. 226.] *The perfect love of God cannot be reached in this world.* [2 Cor. v. 6-9.]

[1] MS. hafe of hafe of.

XI. How we may reach the Love of God in this World.

dum sumus in hoc corpore pergrinamur a Domino, per fidem enim ambulamus, et non per speciem, audemus autem et bonam voluntatem habemus magis pergrinari a corpore et presentes esse ad Deum; et idcirco contendimus, siue absentes siue presentes, placere illi.' Sayne Paule sais þat 'als lange als we ere in þis body, we ere pilgrymes fra oure Lorde,' þat es, we ere absent fra heueñ in þis exile; we go by trouthe, noghte by syghte, þat es, we lyff in trouthe, noghte in bodily felynge; we dare and hase gud wiłt to be absent fra þe body, and be present to Godď, þat es, we for clennes in concyence, and sekire trouthe of saluacyone, dare desyre gastely absence fra oure body by bodily dede, and be present to oure Lorde. Neuer-þe-les, for we may noghte ȝitt, 'þer-fore we stryfe, wheþer we be absent or present, for to plese Hym̄,' and þat es, we stryfe agayne synnes of þe werlde and likynges of þe flesche by desyre to Hym̄, for to bryñ in þis desire ałt thynges þat lettes vs fra Hym̄. ¶ ȝit askes þou wheþer a mañ may haue þis desire contenually in his herte or noghte. Þe thynke nay. As to þis, I may say as me thynke, þat þis desire may be hadď, as for þe vertu and profite of it, in habyte contenualy, bot noghte in wyrkynge ne vsesynge, as by þis ensample: If þou ware seke, þou sulde haue, as ilke mañ hase, a kyndly desire of bodily hele contenualy in thi herte, what so þou dide, wheþer þou slepe or þou wake, bot noghte ay ylyke. For if þou, slepande or elles wakande, thynke of sum werldly thynge, þan hase þou þis desire anely in habite, noghte in wyrkynge; Bot wheñ þou thynkes of þi seknes and of thi bodily hele, þan hase þou it in vssynge. Righte so, gostely, es it of desyre to Godď. He þat hase þis desyre of þe gyfte of Godď, þofe he slepe, or ells thynke noghte of Godď bot of werldly thynges, ȝit he hase þis desyre in habyte of his saule vntiłt he syñ dedly. Bot wheñ he thynkes of Godď, or of clennes of lyffynge, or of þe Ioyes of Heueñ, Than wirkkis his desyre als lange als he kepis his thoghte and his entente to plese Godď, ouþer in prayere or in meditacyoñ or in any oþer gud dede of actyfe lyfe. Thane es it gude þat ałt oþer besynes be for to stire þis desire and vse it be discrecyoñ, now in a dede, now in a-noþer, after we ere disposede and hase grace

In this world we must walk by faith, not by sight.

Neither can the desire of God be always present to us consciously, but it may in habit.

And this habit is exercised in all religious actions.

4

8

12

16

20

24

28

32

36

XI. Good Thoughts help to Religious Feelings.

to. This desire es rute of aƚƚ thi wirkkynges; For, wete þou
wele, whate gude dede it be þat þou+ dose for Godd̄, bodily or   [† Lf. 226 bk.]
gostely, it es ane vsynge of þis desyre; and þer-fore when þou
4 duse a gude dede, or prayes, or thynkis of Godd̄, thynk noghte in
thi herte, doutande wheþer þou desires or noghte, For þi dede
schewes thi desyre. Suɱ ere vnkonande, and wenes þat þay   Some foolish-
desire noghte Godd̄, bot if þay be ay criande ef Godd̄ with   ly think that they cannot
8 wordis of þaire mouthe, or elles in theire hertis by desyrand   have this de-
                                                              sire of God
wordes, as if þay said thus : 'A, Lorde, brynge me to Thi blysse !'   except they are continu-
'Lorde, make me safe !' or swylke oþer. The wordis ere gude,   ally calling upon Him.
wheþer þay be sownned in þe mouthe, or eƚƚs fourmede in þe
12 herte, For þay stire a mans herte to þe desyrynge of Godd̄. Bot
neuer-þe-les, with-owtteɱ any swylke wordes, a clene thoghte of
Godd̄ or of any gostely thynge, as of vertuȝ or of þe manhede
of Criste, of þe Ioyes of Heueɱ, or of vndirstandynge of Haly
16 Writte, with lufe, may be bettire þan slyke wordis. For a clene
thoghte of Godd̄ es sothefaste desyre to Hyɱ; and þe mare
gastely þat thi thoghte es, þe mare es thi desire ; and for-thi be   Good deeds
þou noghte in dowte ne in were when þou prayes or thynkes   prove the ex-
                                                             istence of the
                                                             desire.
20 one Godd̄, or eƚƚs duse any owtwarde dedis to thyne euencristyɱ,
wheþer þou desyres Hyɱ or noghte, For thi dedis schewes it.
Neuer-þe-les, if it be so þat aƚƚ thi gude dedis bodyly and gastely
ere a schewynge of thi desire to Godd̄, ȝit es þer a dyuersite
24 by-twix gastely & bodily dedis ; For dedis of contemplatyfe
lyfe er propirly and kyndly wirkyng of þis desire, bot owtwarde   Especially the
dedis ere noght so ; and for-thi, wheɱ þou prayes or thynkes one   deeds of con-
                                                                  templative
Godd̄, thi desire to Godd es mare hale, mare feruent, and mare   life.
28 gastely, þan wheɱ þou duse oþer dedis vn-to thyne euencristyɱ.

N ow þan, if þou aske how þou saƚƚ kepe this desire and   I will endea-
norische it, a litiƚƚ I saƚƚ teƚƚ the, noghte for þou saƚƚ   vour to tell
                                                              you some-
vse þe same fourme aƚƚ-way as I say, Bot for þou saƚƚ   thing as to
                                                              the way of
32 hafe, if nede be, some wyssyng for to rewle the in thyɱ   nourishing
                                                             this desire.
ocupacyoɱ. For I may noghte, ne I caɱ noghte, teƚƚ
the fully what es beste ay to þe for to vse, Bot I saƚƚ say to þe
sumwhate as me thynke. One nyghtis, aftir thi slepe, if þou
36 wiƚƚ ryse for to serue thi Lorde, thow saƚƚ fele thi-selfe firste

XI. Good Thoughts for Meditation.

fleschely heuy, and sumtyṁ lusty; Than salt þou dispose the for to pray, or for to thynke soṁ gude thoghte for to qwykkyṅ thi herte to Godd, and sett all thi besynes firste for to drawe vp thi thoghte fra werldly vanytes and fra vayne ymagynacyouns fallande in-to thi mynde, þat þou may fele sum deuocyoṅ in thi sayinge, or ells, if þou will thynke of gostely thynges, þat þou be noghte letted with swylke vayne thoghtes of þe werlde or of þe flesche in thi thynkynge. Thare ere many maners of thynkynges: whilke ere beste to þe, I caṅ noghte say, Bot I hope þe whilke þou felis maste sauour in, and maste riste for þe tyme, it es beste

Think over the sins which you have committed. [† Lf. 227.]

for the. Thow may, if þou will, sumtyṁ thynke oṅ thi synnes be-fore donne, and of thi freeltes þat þou fallis in ilke day, and aske mercy † and forgyfnes for thayṁ. Also aftir this þou may

And pray for your fellow-creatures.

thynke of synnes and of wrechidnes of thyṅ euencristeṅ, bodily and gastely, with pete, and of compassioṅ of thayṁ, and cry mercy and forgyfnes for thayṁ als tendirly als iff þay ware thyṅ aweṅ; and þat es a gude thoghte, For I tell þe for-sothe þou may make oþer mens synnes a precyouse oynement for to hele with thyne aweṅ saule when þou hase mynde of thaym.

Which is a precious oint-ment to the soul.

This oynement es precyouse, all if þe spycery in it-selfe be noghte full clene, For it es triacle made of venyṁ for to distroye venyṁ, þat es to saye, thyne aweṅ synnes, and oþér mens also broghte in-to þi mynde. If þou bete þaṁ wele with sorowe of herte, pete and compassioṅ, þay turne vn-to triacle, whilke makes thi saule hale fra pryde and envye, and brynges in lufe & charite to thyne euencristeṅ. This thoghte es gude sumtyme for to hafe.

Also meditate upon the In-carnation of our Lord.

Also þou may hafe mynde of þe manhede of oure Lorde, in his byrthe or in his passioṅ, or in any of his werkes, and fede thi thoghte with gastely ymagynacyoṅ, of it, for to stirre thyne affeccioṅ to mare lufe of Hyṁ. This thoghte es gude and spedfull, namely when it commes frely of Goddes gyfte, with deuocyoṅ and feruour of þe sperite. Elles if a maṅ may noghte lightly hafe sauour ne deuocyoṅ in it, I halde it, noghte spedfull þaṅ to a maṅ for to prese to mekill þare-till, as if he walde gete it by maystry. For he sall mowe breke his heuede; and his body and he sall neuer be þe nerre. For-thi me thynke, vn-to þe it es

XI. Good Thoughts for Meditation.

gude for to hafe in mynde his manhede sumtyme ; and if deuocyoñ and sauour cuɱ with-alle, kepe it and folowe it for a
tyme ; bot leue of sone, and hyng noghte to lange þare-appoñ.
4 Also if deuocyoñ cum noghte with mynde of þe passioñ, stryne
noghte to prese to mekill þare-after. Take esyly þat will cuɱ,
and go furthe to soɱ oþer thoghte. Also, oþer þar bene þat ere
mare gostely, as for to thynke of vertus, and for to se by lyghte
8 of vndirstandynge what þe vertu of mekenes es, and how a maɲ
sulde be meke. Also, what es pacyence and clennes, rightwysnes,
chastyte, and sobirte, and swylke oþer, and how a man sulde gete
all thiese vertus, and by swylke thoghtes for to hafe gret desire
12 and langgyng to þise vertus for to hafe thayɱ, and also for to
hafe a gastely syghte, and þe desyre of þise vertus. A saule sulde
mowe fele grete comforthe if a man had grace of oure Lorde,
with-owtteɲ whilke grace a mans thoghte es halfe blynde, with-
16 owtteɲ sauour of gastely swetnes. Also for to thynke of þe
sayntes of oure Lorde, of Appostills, Martirs, Confessours and
haly virgyns, Byhalde inwardly thaire haly lyffynge, þe grace
and þe vertus þat oure Lorde gafe þaɱ here liffande, and by þis
20 mynde for to stirre thyɲ aweɲ herte to take ensaumpill of þaɱ
vn-to better lyffynge. Also the mynd of oure Lady Saynt Marie
abowne all oþer sayntes, for to see by gostely eghe þe abowndance of grace in hire haly saule, wheɲ scho was here lyffand, þat
24 owre Lorde gafe hir allane, passande † all oþer creatours ; For in
hir was full-hede of all vertus, with-owttyɲ weɱ of synɲ. Scho
had full mekenes and perfit charite, and fully with þise þe bewte
of all oþer vertus so hally, þat þare myghte no styrrynge of
28 pride, envie, ne wrethe, ne fleschely lykynge, ne no manere of syɲ
enter in-till hir herte, ne defoule þe saule in no party of it. The
behaldynge of þe fairehede of þis blyssid saule sulde stirre a
mans herte vn-to gostely comforthe gretly ; and mekill mare þaɲ
32 abowne þis, þe thynkynge of þe saule of Ihesu oure blyssid Lorde,
the whilke was aned fully to þe Godhede, passand with-owttyɲ
comparisoɲ oure Ladye and all oþer creaturs. For in þe persoɲ
of Ihesu er two kyndis, þat es, Godd' & maɲ, fully anede to-
36 gedir. By þe vertu of this blysfull anynge, whilke may noghte

But do not force yourself too much to these thoughts.

Also meditate upon the different virtues.

And on the lives of the Saints, Martyrs, and Confessors.

Specially of our Lady Saint Mary.

[† Lf. 227 bk.

Who had all virtues in perfection.

But above all the character of Jesus, who was a union of God and man.

XI. Good Thoughts for Meditation.

be saide ne consayued'be manes wit, the saule of Ihesu ressayuede þe fulhede of wysedom̃ and lufe and all gudnes, as þe Appostill [Colos. ii. 9.] saise: 'Plenitudo diuinitatis inhabitavit in *ipso corporaliter;*' þat es, þe Godhede was anede fully to þe manhede in þe saule of 4 Ihesu; and so by þe saule duellide in þe body. Þe mynde of þe manhed of oure Lorde on þis wyse, þat es, for to behalde þe vertus and þe ou*er*-passande grace of þe saule of Ihesu, sulde be con- *And of the* fortheabill to a mans saule. Also mynd of þe myghte of þe 8 *great works* *of God.* wysedom̃ & þe gudnes of oure Lorde in all his creaturs, For in als mekill als we may noghte see Godd' fully in hym-selfe, her lyffande, For-thi we sall be-halde hym, lufe hym and dred hym, and wondire hys myghte and his wysdom̃, and his gudnes in his 12 *And of the* werkes and his creaturs. Also for to thynke of þe mercy of oure *mercy which* *the Lord has* Lorde þat he hase schewed to þe and to me, and to all synfull *shewed to us.* kaytyfes þat hase bene combirde in synn̄, speride so lange in þe deuells p*r*esone, how oure Lorde sufferde vs pacyently in oure 16 syn̄, and tuke na vengeance of vs, as he myghte ryghtfully hafe donne, and putt vs till helle, if his mercy had noghte lettide hym̃, Bot for lufe he sparede vs, he had pete of vs, and sente his grace in-till oure hertes, and callid vs owte of oure syn̄, and by 20 his grace hase turnede oure will hally to hym̃, for to hafe hym̃, and for his lufe to for-sake all man*er* of syn̄. The mynde of þis mercy and þis gudnes made, wit*h* oþ*er* circumstance mo þan I can̄ or may reherse, now brynges in-to my saule grete triste in oure 24 Lorde and full hope of saluacyon̄, and it kyndylls desire of lufe *Also meditate* myghtily to þe Ioyes of Heuen̄. Also for to thynke of þe *upon the* *wretchedness* wrechidnes, þe myscheues and þe perills, bodily and gastely, þat *of this life* *and the joys* fallis in þis lyfe, and aft*er* þat, for to thynke of þe Ioyes of 28 *of Heaven.* Heuen̄, how mekill blysse þare es, and how mekill Ioye; For þare es no syn̄, no sorowe, no passion̄, no payne, no hungre, no [† Lf. 228.] thriste, † no sare, no sekenes, no dowte, no drede, no schame, no schenchip*e*, no defaute of myghte, ne lakkynge of lyghte, no want- 32 tynge of will; Bot thare es sou*er*ayne fairenes, lyghtnes, strenghe, Fredom̃, hele, lykynge ay-lastande, wysedom̃, lufe, pees, wirchipe, sekirnes, ryste, Ioy and blysse wit*h*-owtten̄ ende. The more þat þou thynkis and felis þe wrechidnes of þis lyfe the more frequently sall 36

XI. Good Thoughts for Meditation.

þou desire þe Ioye and þe riste of þat blyssede lyfe. ¶ Many men er couetouse of werldly wyrchips and erthely reches, and thynkes nyghte and day, dremande and wakande, how and what maner
4 þay myghte wyn þare-to, and for-getes þe mynde of thaym selfe of þe paynes of helle and of þe Ioyes of Heuen. Sothely þay are noghte wyse : Thay ere lyke vn-to þe childir þat rynnes aftire buttyrflyes, and, for þay luke noghte to thaire fete, þay fall sum-
8 tyme, and brekes þaire legges. What es all þe wirchipe and þe pompe of þis werlde in reches and Iolyte, bot a buttirflye ? Sothely noghte elles, and ȝitt mekill lesse. Thare-fore I praye þe, be þou couetouse of þe Ioyes of Heuen, and þou sall hafe wir-
12 chipe and reches þat euer more sall laste. For at þe laste ende, when werldly couetouse men brynges no gud in thaire handis, (for all þe wirchipes & rechese er turned to noghte saue sorowe and payne,) Than sall heuenly couetous men þat forsakes trewly
16 all vayne wyrchips of þis werlde,—or ells if þay hafe wirchips & reches þay sett noghte þaire lykynge ne þaire lufe in thaym, Bot ay in drede, in meknes, in hope, and in sorowe sumtym, and habydes þe mercy of Godd' paciently,—þay sall þan hafe fully þat
20 þay hase couetid, For thay sall be coround as kynges, and sitt vpe with oure Lorde Ihesu in þe blysse of Heuen. Also þar are many oþer meditacyons, mo þan I kan say, whilke oure Lorde puttis in-to a mans mynde for to stirre þe affeccyon and reson
24 of þe saule to lathe vanytes of þis werlde, and for to desyre þe Ioyes of Heuen. These wordes I saye to þe, noghte as I had fully schewede þese maners of meditacions as þay ere wroght in a manes saule, Bot I touche thaym to þe a lyttill, for þou sulde, by
28 þis littill, vndirstande þe more. Noghte for-thi me thynke it es gude vn-to þe þat, when thou disposeȝ þe for to thynke of Godd' as I hafe be-fore saide, or one oþer wyse, if thi herte be dulle and myrke, and felis noþer witt ne sauour, ne deuocyon for to
32 thynke, bot anely of a naked desyre & a wayke will, þat þou walde fayne thynke of Godd', bot þou can noghte, þan I hope it es gud to þe þat þou stryue noghte to mekill with thi selfe, as if þou walde by thyn awen myghte ouercome † thi selfe, For þou
36 myghte lightely Fall so in-to more myrknes, bot if þou ware þe

Many are eager for the things of this world, like children running after butterflies.

But be thou covetous of the Joys of heaven.

There are many other meditations, which I cannot here enumerate,

If you find your heart dull and dark break off your meditation and say your Pater Noster and Ave, or read your Psalter.

[† Lf. 228 bk.]

XI. Dunger of Excess in Spiritual Exercises.

more slye in thi wirkynge; and for-thi I hald it than moste sekyre vn-to þe for to say thi Pater noster & þine Aue Maria of þi matyns, or ells for to rede apoñ thi sauter, For þat es euer-more a sekyr standarde þat wiłł noghte faile; who-so may cleue 4 þer-to, he saɫɫ noghte erre; and if þou may by prayenge gete deuocyoñ, Thañ, if þi deuocyoñ be anely in affeccioñ, þat es, in a grete desire to Godd' with gastely delyte, halde furthe thi saynge, & brek noghte lyghtely off, For it Fallis þat praynge 8 with þe mouthe getis and kepis feruour of deuocioñ; and if a

If these exercises bring to your heart a devout thought you may entertain it.

mañ cesse of saynge, deuocyoñ vanysche away. Neuer-þe-les, if deuocioñ of prayere brynge to thi herte gastely a thoghte of þe manhed of oure Lorde, or of any oþer before-said, and þis thoghte 12 sulde be lettide by þi saynge, þan may þou cesse of saynge, and ocupye þe in meditacyoñ vntiłł it passe away. ¶ Bot of certayne thynges the by-houes be-warre in þi meditacioñ. Sum saɫɫ I tełł þe. Ane, þat wheñ þou hase had a gastely thoghte, ouþer in 16 ymagynynge of þe manhede of oure Lorde, or of swylke bodily thynges, and þi saule hase bene fedd' and comforthid þer-with,

Yet strive not too much to retain such a thought.

and passes away by þe-selfe, be þou noghte to besy for to kepe it stiłł by maystry, For it saɫɫ þan turne to pyne and to bitternes. 20 Also, if it passe noghte away, bot duellis stiłł in thi mynd' by any traueɫɫ of þi selfe, and þou for comforthe of it wiłł noghte leue it,

And do not suffer it to interfere with your rest or your duties.

and þer-fore it reuys the fra þi slepe on nyghtys, or elles oñ dayes, fra oþer gud dedis, þis es noghte wele, Thou saɫɫ wilfully breke of 24 wheñ [it] askis, ӡa, sumtyme wheñ þou hase maste deuocyoñ, and ware latheste for to leue it, as wheñ it passes resonabiłł tyṁ, or ells it turnes to dissese of thyñ euencristeñ, Bot if þou do so,

It is not with you as with those worldly people who only feel devotion once or twice in a year.

elles þou dusse noghte wysely, as me thynke. A werldly mañ 28 or womañ þat felis noght peraunter deuocyoñ twys in a ӡere, if he felid, by þe grace of oure Lorde, gret compunccyoñ for his synnes, or elles by a mynde of þe passioñ of oure Lorde, þofe he ware put fra his slepe a nyghte, or two or thre, vn-tiłł his heued werke, 32 it es no force, for it commes to þaṁ seldoṁ; Bot to þe, or to a-noþer mañ or womañ þat hase this maner of wirkynge in custoṁ, as ware ilke oþer day, it es spedfułł for tiłł hafe discre-cyoñ in ӡour wyrkynge, noghte fully faɫɫ þer-to for to folow it 36

XI. Learn Humbly of Christ.

als mekill als will com̅. And I halde þat it es gud to þe for to vse þis maner in what deuocyon̅ þat þou be, þat þou hyng noght to lange þare-appon̅, ouþer for to put þe fra thi mete or thi slepe
4 † in tyme, or for to disesse any oþer man̅ vnskilfully. The wyse man̅ sayse, 'Omnia tempus habent.' Þat es, 'all thyngis hase tyme.' Anoþer thyng es this, þat þe by-houys be-warre off. If thi thoghte be ocupied in ymagynacyon̅ of þe manhede of owre
8 Lorde, or in any swilke oþer, and after this þou erte besy with all þe desire of thi herte for to seke knawynge or felyng mare gastely of þe Godhede, prese noghte to mekill þar-after, ne suffire noghte thi herte fall fra þe desire, as if þou ware abydande or
12 gapand aftir sum qwyent stirrynge, or sum wondirfull felynge vthire þan þou hase had. Thou sall noghte do so. It es ynoghe to me and to þe for to haue desyre & langynge to oure Lorde; and if he will, of his fre grace, ouer þis desire, send vs of his
16 gostely lyghte, and opyn̅ oure gostely eghen̅ for to se & knawe more of Hym̅ þan we hafe had be-fore by comon̅ trauell, thanke we Hym þar-of; and if He will noghte, for we er ȝit noghte meke ynoghe, or ells we er noghte disposede by clennes
20 of lyffynge in oþer sydis for to ressayue his grace, Than sall we mekly knawe oure awen̅ syn̅ and wrechednes, and hald vs payed with þe desyre þat we hafe to Hym̅, and with oure comon̅ thoghtes þat may lyghtly fall vndir oure ymagynacion̅,
24 as of oure synns, or of Cristes passion̅, or of swilke oþer ; or ells with prayers of þe sauter, or sum oþer, and loue Hym with all oure hert, þat He will gyff vs þat. If þou do oþer wyse, þou may lyghtly be by-gyled by þe spiryte of oure errour, For it es pre-
28 sumpsion̅, a man̅ by his awen̅ wytt for to prese to mekill in-to knawyng of gastly thynges, bot if he felid plente of grace, For þe wyse man saise þus, 'Scrutator maiestatis opprimetur a gloria.' þat es to say, 'Raunsaker of þe myghte of Godd' and of His
32 Maieste, with-owtten̅ gret clennes and meknes, sall be ouerlayde and oppresside of Hym-selfe [1].' &c⁹ explicit.

Hang not too long upon any one point of devotion.

[† L⁵. 229.]

[Eccles. iii. 1.]

Nor strive to push the imagination too far.

But be humbly instructed of Christ as far as He will teach you.

For it is presumption of our own wit to press too far into divine mysteries. [Prov. xxv. 27.]

[1] The Thornton MS. of this Treatise ends here. The Cambridge MS. has 19 more lines. The British Museum MS. stops considerably short of this. As the ending is marked in the Thornton MS., the additional matter in the Cambridge MS. has not been inserted.

XII.

[THE VIRTUE OF OUR LORD'S PASSION.]

[Thornton MS., Lincoln Cathedral Library, leaf 229, back.]

All men lie under sin, but

Witthou wele, dere Frende, þat þof þou had neuer done syñ with thi bodi, dedly, ne venyaƚƚ, bot anely this þat es called Orygynaƚƚ, (for it es þe firste syñ, and þat es þe lossyng of thy ryght- wysnes whilke þou was mad in,) Suld thou neuer hafe bene safe, if oure Lord Ihesu Criste by his passioñ had noghte delyuerde the, and restorede þe agayne. And þou saƚƚ wit þat þou, be þou neuer so mekiƚƚ a wreche, hafe þou donne neuer so mekiƚƚ syñ, for-sake thi selfe and aƚƚ thi werkes gude & iƚƚ, Cry mercy, and aske anely saluacyoñ by þe vertu of his precyouse passyoñ mekly and tristely, and with-owtteñ dowte þou saƚƚ haf it, and fra this orygynaƚƚ syñ and aƚƚ oþer þou saƚƚ be safe. ȝa, and þou saƚƚ be safe as ane ankir incluse; and noghte anely þou, Bot aƚƚ cristeñ meñ & wymeñ þat trowes appoñ his passioñ, and mekes þaim selfe, knawande þaire wrechidnes, askand mercy and forgyfnes, and þe fruyte of his precyouse passioñ, anely lawand þaim-selfe to þe Sacramentes of haly kyrke, þof it be swa þat þay hafe bene cumbyrde in syñ & with syñ aƚƚ þaire lyfe tyme, and neuer had felyng of gastely sauour or swetnes, or gastely knawynge of Godd, þay saƚƚ, in this faith and in þair gud wiƚƚ, be safe, by þe vertu of þe precyouse passione of oure Lorde Ihesu Criste, and com to þe blysse of Heueñ. See here þe Endles mercy of owre Lorde, how lawe He fallis to þe & to me and to aƚƚ synfuƚƚ caytyfs. 'Aske mercy and hafe it:' Thus said þe prophete in þe persoñ of oure Lorde, 'Omnis enym quicunque invocauerit nomen Domini, saluus erit.' 'Ilk mañ, what þat he be, þat in-calles þe name of Godd, þat es to say, askes saluacioñ by Ihesu and by his passioñ, he saƚƚ be safe.' Bot þis curtasye of oure Lorde, sum meñ takes, and erre safede þer-by; and sum, in traiste of his mercy and his curtasye, lyffes stiƚƚ in þair synnes,

the greatest sins can be forgiven to the true penitent through the Passion of Jesus.

Rom. x. 13.]

But some are beguiled by their knowledge of this mercy into a

XII. *The Way to obtain the Blessings of it.*

& wenys for to hafe it when þam lyst; and þan may þay noghte, *presumptuous trust.*
For þay ere takyn̄ or þay wit, and swa þay dampne þam̄ selfe.
Bot now, sayse þou, if þis be sothe þou wondyrs gretly, for þat I
4 fynde wretyn̄ in sum haly mens saghes. Sum sayse, as I vndir- *How then can some learned men declare that none can be saved who do not love the name of Jesus, when there is hope for all penitent sinners?*
stande, þat he þat can̄ noghte lufe þis blyssed name Ihesu, ne
fynd ne fele in it gastely Ioye and delitabilite, with wondirfull
swetnes in þis lyfe here, ffra þe souerayne Ioy and gastely swetnes
8 in þe blysse of Heuen̄ he sall be aliene, and neuer sall he com̄
þar-to. Sothely þise wordes, when I here thaym̄ or redis þam̄,
stonyes me, and makis me gretly ferd'; For I hope, as þou sayse,
þat many, by þe mercy of Godd, sall be safe, be kepyng of his
12 commandementeȝ and by verray repentance of þaire euyll lyfe
be-fore done, þe wylke felid neuer gastely swetnes ne inly sauour
in þe name of Ihesu or in þe lufe of Ihesu. And for-thi I meruell
me þe more, þat þay say the contrarye here-to, as it semys. Als
16 vn-to þis, I may say, as me † thynke, that theire saynge, if it be [† Lf. 230.] *Their words, if well understood, are true.*
wele vndirstanden̄, es sothe, ne it es noghte contrarie to þat
that I hafe said, For þis name Ihesu es noghte ells for to say one
Ynglische bot 'heler or hele.' Nowe euer-ilk man̄ þat lyffes in
20 þis wrechid lyfe, es gastely seke, For þaire es na man̄ þat lyffis
with-owtten̄ syn̄, whilke es gastely seknes, as Sayn Ihon̄ sayse
of hym-selfe and oþer perfite men̄ thus, 'Si dixerimus quod [1 Joan i. 8.]
peccatum non habemus, ipsi nos seducimus, et c⁰.' 'If we say þat
24 we hafe na syn̄, we begile oure-selfe, and sothefastnes es noghte
in vs.' And for-þi he may neuer fele ne com̄ to þe Ioyes of
Heuen̄, vn-to he first be made hale of þis gostely seknes. Bot
þis gastely may na man̄ haf þat hase vse of reson̄, bot if he
28 desire it and lufe it, and hafe delite þar-in, in als mekill als he
hopis for to get it. Now þe name of Ihesu es noghte elles bot
þis gastely hele. Whare-fore it es sothe þat þay say, þat þar may *For no man can be saved who desires not and loves not salvation, and Jesus is salvation.*
na man̄ be safe bot if he lufe & lyke in þe name of Ihesu; For
32 þar may na man̄ be gastely hale, bot if he lufe and desire gastely
hele; For ryght als a man̄ ware bodily seke, þer ware nane
erthely thyng sa dere ne so nedfull to hym̄, ne so mekill suld be
desyrid of hym̄, als bodily hele (For þofe þou wald gyff hym̄ all
36 þe reches and þe wirchips of þis werlde, and noghte make hym

XII. The Way to obtain the Blessings of Christ's Passion.

hale of þat ȝou myghte, þou plesid hym noghte)—Righte so it
es to a man þat es seke gastely, and felis þe payne of gastely
sekness. Nathyng es so dere, so nedfull, ne so mekill desirid of
hym, als his gastely hele, and þat es Ihesu, withowtten whilke, all 4
þe Ioyes of Heuen may noghte lyke hym. And this es þe skill

It was for this reason that our Lord took that name.

(as I hope) whi oure Lorde, when he tuke mankynde for oure
saluacyon, he walde noghte be called by na name betakenande
his Endles beyng, or his myghte, or his wysdom, or his ryght- 8
wysnes, bot anely by þat that was cause of his commynge, and þat
was saluacyon of mans saule. Whilke saluacion was maste
dere and maste nedfull to man; and þis saluacyon, betakens þis
name Ihesu. Þan bi this it semes, þat þer may na man be safe 12
bot if he lufe Ihesu; For þer may na man be safe bot if he lufe
saluacyon, whilke lufe he may hafe þat lyfes and dyes in þe

Nor can any enjoy heaven who love not this blessed name here.

lawest e degre of charite. Also I may say on a-noþer wyse, þat
he þat can noghte lufe þis blessede nam Ihesu with gastely 16
myrthe, ne enjoye in it with heuenly melodye here, he sall neuer
hafe ne fele in þe blysse of Heuen þat fulhede of souerayne Ioye,
þe whilke he þat myghte in þis lyfe, by habondance of perfite

[† Lf. 230 bk.]

charite, enjoye in Ihesu, sall hafe & fele, † and so may thaire 20

Yet a man can be saved who is in the lowest degree of love.

saynge be vndirstanden. Neuer-þe-les, he sall be safe, and hafe
full mede in þe syghte of Godd, all if he be in þis lyfe in the
laweste degre of charite, by kepyng of Goddes commandementes,
For Criste sayse in the Gospelle, 'In domo Patris mei mansiones 24

[Joan xiv. 2.]

multe sunt.' 'In my fadir house erre many sere dwellynges.'
Sum are for perfite saules, þe whilke in þis lyfe ware fulfillede of
grace of þe Haly Gaste, and sang louynngs to Godd in contemplacion of Hym with wondirfull swetnes and heuennly savour. 28

Some there are of great advances in God's love. These are God's darlings.

Þise saules, for þay hade maste charite, sall haue hegheste mede
in þe blyse of Heuen, For þise ere callid Goddes derlyngs.
Othir saules þat ere in þis lyfe inperfite, and erre noghte disposed
to contemplacyon of Godd, ne had noghte þe fullhede of charite, 32
as apostells or martirs had in þe begynnyng of haly Kirke, þay

Others of lower attainment who are God's friends.

sall haue þe lawere mede in þe blyse of Heuen, For þise er
callede Goddis frendis. Þus callis oure Lorde chosen saules in

[Cant. v. 1.]

haly writt, sayand thus, 'Comedite amici, et inebriamini caris- 36

XII. One Star differeth from another Star. XIII. Prayers.

simi.' 'Mi frendes, ete ȝe; and my derlynges, be ȝe drunkyn.' As if oure Lorde said one þis wyse, ' ȝe þat er my frendis, for ȝe keped my commandmenteȝ, and sett my lufe be-fore þe lufe of þe werlde, and lufed me more þan any oþer erthely thynge, ȝe saft be feedd with gastely fude of þe brede of lyfe. Pot ȝe þat er my derlynges, and noghte anely kepid my commandementis, Bot also of ȝoure awen fre witt fulfillede my consailles, and ouer þat ȝe luffed me anely enterely with alt þe myghtes of ȝoure saule, and brynnede in my lufe with gastely delyte, as did pryncypally þe apostillis & martirs, and alt oþer þat myghte com by grace to þe gyfte of perfeccion, ȝe saft be made drunken with þe freeste wyne in my celer, þat es, þe souereyne ioye of lufe in þe blysse of Heuen.' To the whilke blise he brynge vs, þat boghte vs with his precyouse passion, Ihesu Criste, Goddis sone of Heuen. Amen!

[On leaf 231 is the poem ' ¶ Of Sayne Iohn þe euaungelist,' printed in 'Religious Pieces,' E. E. T. Soc. 1867, pp. 87–94.]

P. 10, l. 9. Wychecrafte.—Thus Roberd de Brunne on the first Commandment:—

Ȝyf þou yn swerde other yn bacyn,
Any chylde madest loke theryn,
Or yn thumbe, or yn cristal,
Wycchecraft men clepen hyt alle.—*Handlyng Synne*, 351.

XIII.

[Two Verse-Prayers to the Virgin Mary.]

[*Harl. MS.* 1002, leaf 61, back.]

(I. 1.)

¶ Quene of parage : paradyse repayred I-wysse,
    lyth of linage : lere me of heuenly blysse,
For þat es wage : þat lastet & neuer may misse.

XIII. Prayers.

(I. 2.)

¶ lady joy[i]nge: reioyce vs, joyles abydynge,
þat of al þynge: comfort[1] is & refreshynge,
Pray þou our kynge: he kepe vs in heuen a comynge.
           Amen. oramus. 4

(II.)

Mary so milde,	Grace to vs hylde;
For luf of þi childe,	with blysse þou vs bylde;
here þo wylde	Fro synne þou vs schilde;
þat prayen þe now!	Amen, for our prowe! 8

[1] 'yng' interlined at end of 'comfort.'

NOTES

The following list of suggested emendations, &c., has been compiled with the help of Dr. Horstman's *Richard Rolle of Hampole*, Vol. I, 1895, and the variant MSS. printed there.

1/5 Latin (La Bigne, *Magna Bibliotheca Patrum*, Cologne, 1622, vol. xv, p. 834, Richardus Pampolitanus Eremita) et statim adoratur oleum effusum.
1/7 Read 'be-mene'.
2/7 MS. Harl. 1022 to it be. Latin: et dum inebriat illam, cadit caro : non potest a sua virtute non deficere.
2/20 Read 'tak ande', i. e. take breath ; Latin : respirat animus.
2/22 Read 'and-es'; Latin : anhelat namque mens superno dulcore, tacta amore conditoris incalescit.
2/27 Read '[m]a[n]e'; Latin: hominem.
4/4 Read so [þay desyre þat] þayre. Latin : sic satiantur, vt desiderent: et sic desiderant, vt desiderium non tollat satietatem.
4/19 Read 'w[ye]t all'; Latin : cognoscant vtique vniuersi.
4/25 Read 'l[i]fe'; Latin : vitam.
4/31 Latin : terra suauiter viuentium.
5/5 Read 'in deserte (Latin : indefesse) fastande, in þe monte anely prayande'.
8/11 Read 'wiþ-takand'. 8/13 Read 'trauayle here. Þay'.
9/1 Read 'for-[thy] þaire'. 9/11 Read 'For'.
9/20 Read 'lyttill hole. Ten ȝere scho'. Latin : Et neque viros neque mulieres unquam videns per annos decem (Migne, *Patrol.* 74. 256).
10/26 'dispyse' may be correct ; cp. 'vanysche ', 42/10, 'rauesche ', 2/26.
11/12 After 'vyces', Horstman inserts the second manner from MS. Arundel 507, 'Sithen speciali, þat we cesse of alle bodili werkis'.
11/28 Read 'barnes, þat es, lande'.
13/25 Read 'gude hope, noghte', so MS. Camb. Dd. v. 64.
14/6 Comma after 'wondyrfull'.
14/8 Read 'gastely. [It is haly] when'.
14/11 Read 'wondirfull, [when] it'.
15/11 Read 'this [anehe]de '; Pepwell's print of 1521, ' this onehede '.
15/17 Read 'Imagy[na]cyones'.
15/30 Read 'so[the]fastenes'.
16/17 Comma after 'maners'.
16/19 Full stop after 'charyte'.
17/19 Read 'Bot [for] a '; MS. Camb. 'bot for þe '.
17/21 Comma after 'vnclennes'.
17/27 Read 'es ofte'; so MS. Camb.
19/26 Read 'kepis [hym] in '; so MS. Camb.
19/35 Read 'es gude'; so MS. Camb.

50   Notes

20/15   Read 'he [be this felynge] and'; so MS. Camb.
20/18   Read 'ymagy[na]cion'.
20/21   Read 'awen [syghte] mare'; so MS. Camb.
22/3   Read 'behouyth to', so Notary's print of 1507.
23/2   Read 'o[f]'; so Notary.
23/26   Read 'se[t]te' (?), i.e. directed; cp. MS. Vernon: 'for hit is
        charite, speciali set in to him'.
23/30   Read 'for-[thi]'; MS. Vernon 'perfore'.
23/32   Read '[vn]discrecion'; so MS. Vernon.
23/33   MS. hatith; cp. 26/19, where there are dots under ti.
24/8   Read 'ordire [of] charite'; so MS. Vernon.
24/19-20 Read 'teche hem [forto] amende'; MS. Vernon 'to'.
25/1   Read 'le[w]ed'; so MS. Vernon.
25/15   Read 'f[len]'; so MS. Vernon, Notary.
26/9   Read '[nott with]stondynge'.
26/29   vn-couthe and: MSS. Vernon, Harl. 2254 omit.
27/12   Read 'of[t]'; so MS. Harl.
27/13   Read 'þ[er]at'; so MSS. Vernon, Harl.
27/27-8 Something has been omitted. Harl. adds after 'inwarde',
        'þat hit was not lettid bi outward dedes for'; so Vernon.
        But Notary adds, after 'hym', 'to shewe it outwarde'.
30/7   luke þam: so MS. Harl.; MSS. Royal, Vernon: loke to hem.
30/17   Read 'for to [thynke lathe for to] leue'; so MS. Vernon; MS.
        Royal omits first 'for to'.
31/8   Semicolon after 'lyfe'.
32/10   Read 'reste [in] deuocyon'; so MSS. Vernon, Royal, Harl.
34/9   Dash after 'wastande'.
34/14   Read 'whare-to [bot] þat'; so MSS. Vernon, Harl.
35/3   Comma after 'bodily'.
35/36   Read 'quoniam'.
36/34   Read 'all o[ure]'; so MS. Vernon.
37/7   Read 'criande [on] Godd'; so MSS. Vernon, Harl.
38/15   Read 'and compassion'.
38/29   No comma after 'ymagynacyon'.
38/33   "   "   "   'halde it'.
38/35   "   "   "   'heuede'; comma after 'body'.
39/4   Read 'stryue'.
39/13   MS. Vernon reads 'siȝt of þe þreo principal vertues:' of troupe,
        hope, & charite. Be þe siȝt & þe disyre', &c.; so MS. Harl.
40/8   Comma after 'myghte'.
41/4   Comma after 'selfe'.
41/32   Omit 'of'; so MS. Vernon.
42/3   Read 'or þi matyns'; so MS. Harl.; Vernon 'or elles'.
42/19   Read 'and [it] passes away by [it]-selfe'; so MSS. Vernon, Harl.
42/23   Omit comma after 'dayes'.
42/25   Read 'when [tyme] askis'; so MSS. Vernon, Harl.
42/35   Read 'as [it] ware'; so MS. Vernon.
45/27   Read 'gastely [hele] may'.
46/1   Read '[i]f þat'.
47/18   Read 'repard', enclosed; cp. Song of Sol. iv. 12.
48/3   Read 'wonynge'.
48/4   Read 'oremus'.

GLOSSARY AND INDEX

ACCIDIE, *n.*, sloth, 23/8.
Accordandly, *adv.*, accordingly, 8/32.
Acostom, *n.*, habit, 20/10.
Active and Contemplative Life, 21-43.
Afforces, *v.*, make strong, 8/20.
Aknowe, *v.*, be a., confess, 33/8.
All if, even if, 46/22.
Alsonne, immediately, 14/27.
Althirhegeste, *adj. superl.*, highest of all, 1/15.
And ... and, both ... and, 31/32.
Ane, anely, anelynes—alone, loneliness: 'by myn ane,' by myself, 5/4, 5, 11, 20/15.
Anede, *pp.*, united, 39/35, 40/4; anehede, 16/1.
Anehede, *n.*, oneness, union, 15/10.
Ankir incluse, enclosed hermit, 44/14.
Anynge, *n.*, union, 39/36.
Araysede, *a.*, raised, high, 13/20.
Arett, *v.*, ascribe, 33/9.
Aristotle on bees, 8/18; on birds, 8/32.
Arraynge, *n.*, arraying, decoration, 29/36.
Astronomyenes, *n.*, astrologers, 10/15.
At, *prep.*, with, 30/14, 21.
At, *conj.*, that, 35/7.
Athe, *n.*, oath, 10/31; *g.s.* athes, 11/4.
Austyn, St., 13/18, 34/25.
Awe, *v.*, owe, ought, 11/17.

Bee, Hampole on its nature, 8-9.
Begynnynge, *a.*, 21/7.
Be-mene, *v.*, mean, 1/7.
Besynes chargis, *n.*, burdens of business, 25/13.
Beyng, *n.*, existence, 46/8.
Bishops and the mixed life, 27.

Bot, *conj.*, except, 1/19; bot if, unless, 42/27.
Bouxomnes, *n.*, obedience, duty, 11/25.
Breke of, *v.*, break off, stop, 42/24.
Brennande, *a.*, burning, 15/21.
By-houely, *a.*, befitting, 28/2.
By-houys, *v.*, should, ought to, 5/15.
Bylde, *v.*, defend, 48/6.

Cesarius, tales by, 6/28, 7/14.
Charge, *n.*, heaviness, 9/13.
Chargede, *pp.*, loaded, burdened, 9/16.
Charemynge, *n.*, working by charms, 10/9.
Chese, *v.*, choose, 5/19.
Cheson, *n.*, reason, good cause, 10/25.
Christ's Passion, Virtue of, 44-7.
Clerete, *n.*, clarity, clearness, 18/20.
Coal, how to light, 32/25-31.
Commandments, the Ten, 10-12.
Comonynge, *n.*, communion with, 17/25.
Compleccionne, *n.*, embracing, fleshly intercourse, 14/16.
Contrition, imperfect and perfect, 6-7.
Coryous, *a.*, over inquisitive, 3/11.
Couaytabill, *a.*, 3/30.
Couaytes, *n.*, covetousness, 14/24.
Cun thanke, give thanks, 29/34.
Cuppillynge, *n.*, joining, 35/24, 25.

Ded, dede, *n.*, death, 2/1, 13/19.
Defaile, *v.*, lack, 2/8.
Delighting in God, 14.
Delitabilite, *n.*, 45/6.
Delycyousely, *adv.*, luxuriously, 6/30.
Desederabill, *a.*, desirable, 2/28.
Desyrand, *a.*, desiring, longing, 37/8.

52 Glossary and Index

Devil in shape of a woman, 6/9.
Divining by stars, &c., 10/14.
Drawes, *v.*, pulls up, 3/12.
Drede, *n.*, fear; "na drede þat ne þay ere," 'no fear but that they are,' 4/18.
Duse, *v.*, do, 12/12, 13.
Dyscryuede, *pp.*, described, 17/4.

Eggyng, *n.*, egging, temptation, 13/29.
Elde, *n.*, old age, 11/24.
Enchesone, *n.*, reason, cause, 7/4.
Enforssede, *v.*, forst, 3/22.
Enforthis, *v.*, enforces, 2/23.
Enjoye, *v.*, rejoice, 46/17.
Er, *v.*, are, 43/18; erre, 35/29.
Even, equally with, 23/28; MS. Vernon, aȝeynes.
Eysede, *pp.* = oysede, used, directed, 14/32.
Ezechiel the prophet, 17/29.

Falles, *v.*, happens, 2/7.
Famyliare till, *a.*, familiar with, 7/3.
Fand, *v.*, found, 4/29.
Felide, sowne es, sound is perceived, 19/13.
Fette, *n.*, feet, 8/6.
Files, *v.*, defile, foul, 4/18.
Fillynge, *n.*, filling, fullness, 4/3, 5.
Fire, how to make a, 32/25-31.
Flyghyng, *n.*, power of flight, 8/33, 34, 9/3.
Forbrekes, *v.*, utterly breaks, 18/26.
Force, *n.*, care, 28/30.
Forthe dayes, late in the day, 9/27.
For-thy, *adv.*, therefore, 9/23.
Fremmede, *a.*, unconnected by blood, strange, 8/23.
Full, *adj.*, foul, 7/16.
Full-hede, *n.*, fullness, 39/25.
Fychede, *v.*, pierced; thurghe-fychede, pierced through, 2/4.

Gastely, *a.*, ghostly, spiritual, 45/6, 7, 13.
Ger, *v.* make, cause, 32/26.
Gernyng, *n.*, yearning, 14/5.
Gillery, *n.*, trickery, cheating, 12/10. (Still in use in Lincolnshire.)
Grauynge, *n.*, burial, 7/1.
Gregory, St., 26/23.

Gretynge, *n.*, crying, grieving, 5/10.
Greuesnes, *n.*, grievousness, 3/15.
Gruchynge, *n.*, grudging, grumbling, 32/19.

Habedyn, *pp.*, abided, waited, 32/29.
Hampole's temptation, 5-6.
Haunten, *v.*, deal with, handle, 21/5.
Haver, *n.*, possession, property, 26/2.
Hegheynge, *n.*, uplifting, 14/18.
Heldede, *v.*, hylde.
Hele, *n.*, salvation, 1/15.
Heleful, *a.*, healthful, 4/20.
Heraclides, tale by, 9/17.
Holy Ghost's gifts, 13.
Hope, *v.*, think, 28/5, 38/9.
Hungres thaym, they hunger (for more), 3/29.
Hurtynge, *n.*, 11/33.
Hyghte, *v.*, promised, 7/4.
Hylde, *v.*, pour out, bestow, 48/5; *pt.*, heldede, inclined, 7/9.

Illumynede, *pp.*, 17/9.
Images to be honoured, 10/21.
In, *prep.*, for, 9/34.
In-calles, *v.*, invokes, 44/28.
Indiscrecyon, *n.*, 19/10.
In-ȝettis, *v.*, pours in, 3/13.
In-ȝettynge, *n.*, inpouring, 4/9.
Inglysce, *n.*, English, 1/4.
Inlastande, *pr. p.*, lasting, 3/15.
Inlawes (Harl. MS., insawes), *v.*, plants or sows in, 3/13; Lat., inserit.
Inly, *a.*, inward, 45/13.
Inryses, *v.*, springs, 2/25.
Intermettid, *v.*, mixt, occupied, 27/14.
Israel = a man seeing God, 32/1, 3.
It, itself, 19/24.

Jacob, 32/1, 2.
Jacob and Laban, Rachel and Leah, 30-1.
Jesus, the name, 1-5.
Ioyeynge, *n.*, merriment, 5/10.

Kelis, *v.*, cools, 20/6.
Kennede, *v.*, made to know, taught, 17/28.
Kyndely, *a.*, natural, 15/20.

Glossary and Index 53

Langes, v., impers, we long, 3/26.
Languessande, languishing, 2/18, 19.
Lappid, pp., wrapped, 5/1. (Still in use in Lincolnshire.)
Lare, n., lore, instruction, 14/22.
Lathe, v., loathe, 41/24.
Lathynge, n., loathing, 34/30, 35/5, 16.
Laude, = lande, 11/28.
Lawand, pr. p., humbling, subjecting, 44/18.
Lawlyly, adv., humbly, 11/27.
Layery, a., filthy, 14/23.
Leche, v., heal, 2/4; n., healer, 2/18.
Lelely, adv., loyally, truly, heartily, 3/7.
Lere, v., teach, 47/19.
Lessynge, n., diminution, 4/8.
Lettys, v., hinder, 11/12.
Leuefully, with permission, 21/6.
Lichoure, n., lecher, 12/1.
Lofe, v., praise, 9/31; loues, 20/4.
Loute, v., worship, 10/7, 20, 23.
Louynge, n., praise, 10/2, 17/18.
Lowuabyll. a., praiseworthy, 3/8.
Lufabyll, a., lovable, 2/28.
Luke, v., look after, care for, 30/7.
Lya, Leah, 31/2, 7, 13, 28.
Lyenges, n., lies, 12/17.
Lyth, light, glorious, 47/19.

Maria, 24/24.
Martha, 24/16.
Mary, our Lady Saint, 39/21.
Mawmetryse, n., idolatrous practices, 10/9.
Maystry, n., violence, force, 38/35.
Medfull, a., rewardful, 28/6.
Medefully, adv., profitably, 24/28.
Medle, v., mix, mingle, 24/14; medled, 26/28, 27/6; medlid, 24/34, 26/35: medelid, 25/23.
Mekes, v., humble, 44/16.
Mellynge, n., meddling, 32/20.
Menes, n., things interposed, 18/3.
Mengede, v., mingled, mixed, 1/20.
Merghlyere, adv., more thoroughly, Lat. medullitus, 2/5.
Me thynke, it appears to me, 29/28.
Mett, n., measure, 12/11.
Mirke, a., dark, 22/8.

Mobylls, n, movables, goods, 12/24.
Mowe, v., may, can, 22/8; be able to, 38/35, 39/14.
Mynd, remembrance, 39/21; mynde, 5/18.
Myrknes, n., darkness, 41/36.
Myssawe, n., mis-saying, want of respect, 11/26.
Myster, n., need, 13/8.

Nane, a., no, 2/29.
Nakede mynde, simple perception, 20/12, 18.
Nedys, adv., of necessity, 5/15.
Nerehand, adv., nearly, 2/6.
Nerre, adv., nearer, 15/25.
Neuennyd, v., spoken, named, 5/21.
Noghte for-thi, nevertheless, 17/36.
Nourish (feed) the fire with sticks, 33/28.
Noye, n., sorrow, annoyance, disgust, 3/16, 4/7; v., do harm, 12/18.

Of, prep, with, 3/16.
Okyre, n., extortion, usury, 12/11.
Onane, adv., anon, at once, 32/30.
Oneness of God with Man's soul, 15-20.
Oo, a., one, 24/16.
Ouerganger, n., overcomer, 31/5, 35.
Ouer-heghede, v., carried too high, 8/7.
Ouer-hille, v., cover over, 32/27.
Ouerlaide, pp., covered over, 22/5.
Ouer-passande, a., exceeding, 40/7.
Ouertrauells, v., overworks, 18/25.
Owt-ȝettede, pp., poured out, 1/4.
Oys, n., use, 12/4.

Parage, n., high rank, 47/18.
Paris, a wicked Canon at, 6/30; a forgiven scholar at, 7/16.
Payede, pp., contented, 15/1.
Peraunter, adv., peradventure, 42/29.
Perré, n., jewellery, 29/9.
Plentivosly, adv., plenteously, 24/23.
Poure, a., pure, 8/21.
Prelaci, n., office, post of a bishop, 27/24, 29; pl., 27/18.
Presumpsion, n., 43/27-8.

Glossary and Index

Priste, priest, 33/19.
Profette, v., advanced, 6/14.
Prow, n., profit, 13/27.
Pryncypally, adv., chiefly, specially, 47/9.
Pure, adv., poorly, 4/32.
Purede, pp., purified, 18/1.
Put, v., ascribe, 33/13.
Pyne, n., sorrow, 42/20.

Quemfull, a., pleasing, 34/31.
Qwyent, a., quaint, curious, 43/12.

Rachel, 30/36, 31/3, 8, 10, 28.
Raunsaker, n., investigator, 43/31.
Rauyschynge, n., ecstasy, 17/21.
Redies, v., preparest, 3/2.
Refreynynge, n., bridling, restraining, 22/20.
Repressynge, n., 14/17.
Reue, v., draw away, steal, 8/20.
Rewarde, n., regard, care, 26/19.
Rusynngs, n., boastings, 19/4.
Ruysand, v., praising (himself), 13/25.

Sadely, adv., firmly, 15/15.
Saghes, n., saws, doctrines, teaching, 45/4.
Saint Gregory, 26/23.
St. Paul on body and spirit (1 Cor. xi. 8, 9 ; xv. 46), 21/12-16.
St. Victor, the Abbey of, at Paris, 7/19.
Sandes, n., ordinances, 15/1.
Sare, n., disease, 40/31.
Sare-eghede, a., sore-eyed, 31/10.
Sauoure, n., relish, delight, 3/14.
Sauyre,v., experience,1/20 ; sauour, 20/28.
Schenchippe, n., disgrace, 40/32.
Scholar at Paris, forgiven his sins, 7/16-34.
Seke to þe dede, sick unto death, 6/31.
Sekerly, adv., securely, 5/18.
Sensualite, n., the senses, 14/26, 16/22, 23, 27, 29.
Sentence of dampnacyone, 7/12.
Sere, a., several, various, 9/7 ; separate, 46/25.
Serely, adv., separately, 13/10.
Sese, v., see, 4/2.
Sesse of, cease from, 11/12.

Seven Gifts of the Holy Ghost, 13.
Sithen, adv., afterwards, 22/2.
Skilfully, adv., according to reason, 26/10.
Skyll, n., reason, 14/28, 32.
Slaers, n., slayers, 11/34.
Slokynns, v., slackens, quenches, 3/10.
Slyke, a., such, 37/16.
Smites his sins, Holy Writ, 13/22.
Sobbynge, n., 7/20.
Socerye, n., sorcery, 10/13.
Softly living, the land of, 4/31.
Somdele, a., partial, 18/20.
Sothely, adv., truly, surely, in sooth, 1/7.
Souple, a., supple, flexible, 21/11.
Sownnande, pr. p., sounding, speaking, 1/19.
Specyalle, n., intimate friend, object of love, 5/20.
Spedfull, a., profitable, 28/6.
Spendide, pp., spent, 28/29.
Speride, pp., shut up, enclosed, 40/15.
Spycery, n., spices, 38/20.
Stallworthely, adv., strongly, violently, 6/6.
Stere, v., guide, 26/23.
Sternys, n., stars, 10/14.
Sticks = good works of active life, 32/36.
Stonyes, v., astonish, overwhelm, 45/10.
Stork or strucio, that can't fly, 9/12.
Strenyde, v., strained, squeezed, 6/6.
Strenghe, v., strengthen, 34/17.
Strength, v., strengthen, 23/17.
Strobillynge, n., trouble, distraction, 23/23.
Strucyo, n., stork, 9/12.
Stryne = stryue, strive, 39/4.
Styrrynges, n., suggestions, 11/9.
Swearing, three ways of sinning in, 10/26.
Swylke, a., such, 11/28.
Sybbe, a., near in blood, 8/22.
Syghynge, n., sighing, 7/20.
Syngulere, a., s. purpos, purpose of living alone, 5/24.
Sythes, n., times ; ofte-sythes, oftentimes, 8/28.

Glossary and Index

Taa, tan, toþer, one, other, 31/30, 32.
Tagillynge, n., entangling, 14/10.
Tagyld, pp., entangled, 13/12.
Takynnynge, n., token, mark, seal, 1/23.
Tane, þe, and þe toþer, the one and the other, 30/22.
Tempede, pp., tempted, 9/22.
Temptid, n., tempted folk, 5/17.
Ten Commandments, 10-12.
Tene, n., sorrow, misery, 8/28.
Tente to, pp., attended to, cared for, 29/22.
Ternynge, n., turning, 14/26.
Þar, there, 45/30.
That, pron., whoever, 3/28; swyche that = such as, 25/11-12.
Þire, these, 10/17, 33/1; þaire, 10/22.
Þofe, conj., though, 36/28; thoffe, 23/21.
Tholemodnes, n., patience, 9/32.
Thriste, n., thirst, 5/3, 40/31.
Thristis thaym, they thirst (for more), 3/29.
Thristy, a., thirsty, 34/32.
Thythen, adv., thence, 2/24.
Tothire, a., second, 10/24.
Traiste, n., trust, 19/25.
Transfourmynge, n., 16/15.
Trauellynge, n., labour, 18/26.
Trauyliouse, a., laborious, active, 31/7.
Triacle, n., salve, unguent, 38/21, 24.
Tristely, adv., trustfully, 44/12.
Trouthe, n., troth, faith, 36/7.
Trubylyere, a., more troubled, 32/21.
Turment, pp., tormented, 5/2.

Vmbethynke, v., remember 11/10.
Vnauyssedly, adv., foolishly, 11/26.
Vnbuxomnes, n., insubordination, disobedience, 21/10.
Vn-cessandly, adv., unceasingly, 3/23.
Vn-chastely, adv., 6/30.
Vn-couthe, a., unknown, 26/29.
Vndevocyone, n., 11/5.
Vndiscrete, a., 18/35.
Vnhoneste, n., impropriety, 11/26.

Vnkepide, a, 29/22.
Vnkonande, a., ignorant, 37/6; vnkunnynge, 26/29.
Vnletterede, a., uneducated, 33/29.
Vnmyghtty, a., weak, 11/24.
Vnnethes, adv., scarcely, hardly, 2/5.
Vnordaynde, a., unregulated, 14/30.
Vn-perfitte, a., incomplete, 6/27.
Vnrewled, a., unregulated, 23/29.
Vnskillwyse, a., unreasonable, 16/7.
Vn-to, to, 34/15.
Vnwysse, a., unwise, 3/3.
Vssynge, n., use, 36/27.

Vagacyone, n., wandering, 15/15.
Vilte, n., vileness, 13/24.
Virgin Mary, Two Prayers to, 47.
Virtues of Jesus' name, 1-5.
Vis, n., sight, 35/31; vys, 35/28. MSS. Vern., Harl., vse.

Wem, n., spot, blemish, 39/25.
Wende, v., thought, 31/1.
Were, n., doubt, 37/19.
Werke, v., ache, pain, 42/32.
Wiele, adv., well, 19/21.
Witchcraft, 47.
With-takand, v., reproving, 8/11.
Witterly, adv., utterly, entirely, completely, 27/9.
Woman, Devil as a, tempts Hampole, 5-6.
Wondyrde, pp., astonisht, 6/2.
World of worlds, 6/17.
Wrethe, v., anger, 13/30.
Wyete, v., know, 4/30.
Wyn, v., obtain, win, 11/27.
Wyseleere, adv., more wisely, 34/29.
Wyssyng, n., teaching, 37/32.

Yevynge, v., giving, 23/31.
Ymagy[na]cion, n., imagining, 20/18.
Ympnes, n., hymns, 19/32.
Ynesche, prep., towards, 8/22.

ʒa, yea, 2/27.
ʒarenande, pr. p., yearning for, 2/14.
ʒede, v., went, 4/26.
ʒernynge, n., yearning, desire, 2/15.
ʒitt, adv., yet, 7/24.

The manufacturer's authorised representative in the EU for product safety is Oxford University Press España S.A. of El Parque Empresarial San Fernando de Henares, Avenida de Castilla, 2 - 28830 Madrid (www.oup.es/en or product.safety@oup.com). OUP España S.A. also acts as importer into Spain of products made by the manufacturer.
Printed and bound by CPI Group (UK) Ltd, Croydon, CR0 4YY

20/03/2026

02075337-0001